'Although I've met many healers over the years, Seka is truly exceptional. She has helped many people all over the world with her amazing ability. She's a remarkable person with a very special gift.'
Paul McKenna

'A friend of mine introduced me to Seka over a decade ago. I asked, "What exactly does she do?" And he replied, "Oh, you'll see." I still don't really know what it is exactly, I just know that I feel much better, and I recommend Seka to all my friends. Seka has a special gift, and a no-nonsense approach to healing. We all run on energy, and it's our most precious asset.'
Joely Richardson

'Seka has knowing where most of us operate from belief. The difference is that, through her life experience and exposure to thousands of grateful clients, she has refined an already impressive gift for healing into a profound and unique approach to life itself. There is certainty in her words and knowledge that only comes with maturity and wisdom, the refinement of a life given to healing.'
Dr Anthony Soyer, The Diagnostic Clinic, London

YOU KNOW MORE
THAN YOU THINK

YOU KNOW MORE THAN YOU THINK

HOW TO ACCESS YOUR SUPER-SUBCONSCIOUS POWERS

SEKA NIKOLIC

WITH SARAH TAY

HAY HOUSE

Australia • Canada • Hong Kong • India
South Africa • United Kingdom • United States

First published and distributed in the United Kingdom by:
Hay House UK Ltd, 292B Kensal Rd, London W10 5BE. Tel.: (44) 20 8962 1230;
Fax: (44) 20 8962 1239. www.hayhouse.co.uk

Published and distributed in the United States of America by:
Hay House, Inc., PO Box 5100, Carlsbad, CA 92018-5100. Tel.: (1) 760 431 7695 or
(800) 654 5126; Fax: (1) 760 431 6948 or (800) 650 5115. www.hayhouse.com

Published and distributed in Australia by:
Hay House Australia Ltd, 18/36 Ralph St, Alexandria NSW 2015.
Tel.: (61) 2 9669 4299; Fax: (61) 2 9669 4144. www.hayhouse.com.au

Published and distributed in the Republic of South Africa by:
Hay House SA (Pty), Ltd, PO Box 990, Witkoppen 2068. Tel./Fax: (27) 11 467 8904.
www.hayhouse.co.za

Published and distributed in India by:
Hay House Publishers India, Muskaan Complex, Plot No.3, B-2, Vasant Kunj, New
Delhi – 110 070. Tel.: (91) 11 4176 1620; Fax: (91) 11 4176 1630. www.hayhouse.co.in

Distributed in Canada by:
Raincoast, 9050 Shaughnessy St, Vancouver, BC V6P 6E5. Tel.: (1) 604 323 7100;
Fax: (1) 604 323 2600

The authors of this book do not dispense medical advice or prescribe the use of
any technique as a form of treatment for physical or medical problems without the
advice of a physician, either directly or indirectly. The intent of the authors is only
to offer information of a general nature to help you in your quest for emotional
and spiritual wellbeing. In the event you use any of the information in this book for
yourself, which is your constitutional right, the authors and the publisher assume no
responsibility for your actions.

A catalogue record for this book is available from the British Library.

ISBN 978-1-84850-221-5

Printed in the UK by CPI William Clowes Ltd, Beccles, NR34 7TL.

All of the papers used in this product are recyclable, and made from wood grown
in managed, sustainable forests and manufactured at mills certified to
ISO 14001 and/or EMAS.

In memory of my mother

Thanks to all of you who shared with me your lovely stories that helped make this book happen.

Contents

Foreword

I have had the opportunity to meet many healers over the course of my life and it's my belief that Seka Nikolic is exceptional, which is perhaps why so many people, with such a vast array of problems, go to her for help.

What is particularly interesting is that healing can take place over distance. I had a personal experience of this some years ago when I hurt my knee skiing. I was bored sitting in the chalet, so I called a few friends, one of them being Seka. I believed at the time I had to be in the presence of the healer for it to work. However, Seka asked me to hang up and notice what happened. What followed was extraordinary: I could suddenly feel the pain disappearing from my leg.

I began looking into the research on distance healing and found evidence to support its effectiveness. Randolph C. Byrd, MD, conducted a study into the effects of distance healing through prayer, with fascinating results. What is particularly interesting is that people in the control group, who were not even aware that they were receiving distance healing, experienced significant health improvements. There are numerous scientific studies that show that energy healing works – everything from lowered blood pressure to the hastened healing of wounds, decreased headaches and tumours shrinking has been reported in different scientific papers. It seems we all possess the ability to heal others, and ourselves to some degree.

The notion of the concentration of energy having a therapeutic effect is not a new one, though it struggles to be accepted. But then it was only a few years ago that hypnosis, acupuncture and other 'alternative' treatments were widely considered hocus pocus, and they are almost mainstream these days.

I am not aware of any particular procedure or drug that works for everyone and every malady on every occasion. Psychologist Dr Roger Callahan famously says, 'Anyone who claims a 100 per cent success rate doesn't have enough clients.' However, there are healers who stand out. I have known and worked with Seka for more than 20 years and have seen her help people, many of them sceptical, with all sorts of different problems, and consistently get extraordinary results. In this book, she explains how you can start to discover and utilize your own natural healing abilities. It will give you a valuable insight into her work and a good idea of how her approach will be of help to you. I hope that reading it will open your mind to new life-enhancing possibilities.

Enjoy the journey!

Paul McKenna

Introduction

I was sitting in an airport, waiting to board a plane, when I had an overwhelming urge to give my earrings to the woman sitting next to me. It was such a strong feeling that I didn't question it. I liked my earrings, but wasn't particularly attached to them, and so I took them off and handed them to the bemused stranger.

I explained to her that I didn't quite know why I was giving them to her but I just felt it was the right thing to do. I felt as if they belonged to her.

When I told her this, the grateful lady welled up with emotion and started crying. She told me that her mother had given her a pair of earrings exactly like mine but that she had lost them. When she had sat next to me she had noticed my earrings straightaway and it had made her think of her mother.

We were both overwhelmed.

Most people would say that this strange interaction was due to coincidence, a one-in-a-million chance. But this woman's story is an example of what happens when we listen to, and act on, the messages that we pick up through our energy frequencies. Neither of these women acted consciously; the message was exchanged between them energetically.

Although it might seem like a magical story, things like this happen to all of us every day. Do you ever call someone and, before they even speak, know that they are upset? Or do you ever walk into a room and within a split second know that something is wrong? Maybe you can sense when someone is thinking about you. Have you ever telephoned someone just as they were about to ring you? Or received an email from a friend about whom you dreamed the night before? Can you sense when someone is looking at you from across a room? And can you ever tell what someone is thinking? When you experience situations like these that are hard to explain, it seems that there is more going on than just coincidence. There is: you are experiencing an energetic connection with another person.

Energy is all around you all the time. You can't see it, but right now, this very second, you are surrounded by invisible communication channels. And just as you have your own phone number, passport number and DNA fingerprint, so you have an energetic frequency that distinguishes you from other people, and this creates a worldwide web of energy between you and everyone else, and even between you and objects. So, whilst you pick up messages from people through their words and actions, more importantly, you also *send* and *receive* information through your energy.

Having shared my healing knowledge and experiences in my first book, I wanted to write a book about energy because it is so important in all of our lives. We all know this, even if we're not always conscious of it. Phrases such as 'we're on the same wavelength', 'you're so in tune with each other', 'the atmosphere was electric', 'he sent shivers down my spine', 'they got a good feeling about it' or 'I feel that we're in synch' all describe the innate gift each of us has to communicate energetically. We often call this 'intuition' or 'gut instinct'.

You use your own energetic gift all the time, even if you're not aware of it. What you may also not be aware of right now is that you have a choice over whether or not to connect to a particular energy. You can choose to *receive* the energies that are right for you and protect yourself against the frequencies that are negative for you, and you can also choose what you *send* out to others to attract things that will make your life happy and nourishing.

Each of us is born with this gift, so in this book I shall simply be reminding you of what you already know. I'll be showing you how to become aware of energetic frequencies so that you will be able to reconnect with the powers with which you were born and improve your health, relationships, career and happiness. When you fine-tune your energetic gift, you can bring magic into your life...

PART ONE

THE ENERGETIC WORLD

CHAPTER 1

Energy in Practice: My Life Story

Before you start to learn more about how to use energy in your own life, I thought it would be useful for you to read about some of the experiences I've had and how they have brought me to where I am now.

To begin with, my life followed a similar path to that of most people: I grew up, was educated, began working and started my own family. My mother died tragically in a car accident when I was 19, but apart from that everything seemed 'normal'. I didn't realize at that point that my life was about to change and would never be the same again...

It was a cold wintry day and I made my way to work through heavy snow. I arrived at my office and, as on any other ordinary day, I got to my desk, checked my messages and started to plough through the list of phone calls and piles of paper. Mid-morning, one of my colleagues brought me a document that needed my signature. As I handed back the paper to him, I was compelled to place my hands on his shoulders. I seemed to be controlled by a force that I couldn't explain. I wasn't consciously thinking about what I was doing; I was being guided by a deep instinct.

This man suffered from an acute spinal deformity that caused his back to curve very severely. The movement of his legs was limited and he was confined to a wheelchair. I didn't know him very well and I had never thought or felt anything about him that was out of the ordinary, so I have no idea why, on that particular day, I reached out to help him. It didn't cross my mind to question what was happening – it was as if I couldn't question it. I just laid my hands on his shoulders.

I kept my hands on him for about ten minutes. He was getting hotter and hotter throughout this time and sweating heavily. He was clearly anxious and uncomfortable – but if only he had known how much agony I was in. The pain shot through my hands, up my arms and down my spine. But I was so connected to the energy that I carried on being guided by a force that I knew was bigger than me. It was as if someone else had taken over my body. I also started to see things in my mind about his life that I could never have known.

After what seemed like forever, I lifted my hands from his shoulders. The pain disappeared from my body straightaway, as if someone had flicked a switch. He stood up and looked down at his legs – and then looked at me in horror. He turned his back on me and once he was at a safe distance, he ran out of my office doors, shouting, 'I can walk! I can walk!'

I had just had my first healing experience.

Within minutes, people from all over the building rushed up to me. All I could hear was them shouting out their problems, asking me to help them. Nobody asked me if I was all right. Nobody even asked me what had happened – they all just wanted a piece of me.

It's so hard to put into words how I felt. I had no idea what I'd done or why I'd done it. Had I become something or someone else?

From that moment on, my life changed. The news spread and the media were like animals scrapping to get my story; even my closest friends thought of how I could help them rather than how they could support me. I felt alienated from my body and desperately wanted to run away from my power. I wanted to hide from the attention, to curl up and pretend it wasn't happening, but I didn't. I now know that if I'd reacted like that, I wouldn't be where I am today. My gift was a part of me. I couldn't fight it and I couldn't run away. I couldn't escape this. I had no choice but to go with it.

As my gift developed, my senses became unbelievably strong. It was as if I could feel, hear, smell and see with an astuteness and clarity that I'd never known before. I would pass people on the street and hear their thoughts. I couldn't stop myself. But I had enough to deal with without hearing about everyone else's problems. I felt as though I was slowly going mad.

This awakening made me realize that as well as being able to use healing energy to work on people individually, I was also able to pick up the information that was all around me. This ability became clearer and stronger as I grew accustomed to my gift, but I decided not to use it professionally. I eventually learned to close myself off to it, as I couldn't have coped with being bombarded with all this information and I would also have got drained very quickly. I had a gift to heal people – and it was this power that I decided to develop.

Understanding Is Key

For the first few years after this turning point, I didn't know exactly what was going on or how to cope. A number of times I went to bed at night and hoped that I'd wake in the morning and discover that it had all been a dream, but instead I woke up each day still with my gift, so I knew I had to learn to deal with it.

I really wanted to understand what was happening to me. I didn't want to feel that this power was in control of me – I wanted to be in control of it. But I couldn't even take the pain away from my own body during the treatment. It wasn't mine to carry, but when I treated people, I absorbed it for that period.

People used to say I was performing miracles or that I'd been 'chosen', but I knew I couldn't allow myself to get carried away by that. I needed to keep sight of who I was and who I had always been. I needed to stay down to earth.

All of this happened several years after my mother's tragic accident and in my head I kept asking her to help me. I was sure that she would be able to understand what was happening to me and would know how to cope. I felt that she was my only comfort. I could feel her energy and sense her guidance, but ultimately I knew I had to face the fact that I was in this on my own.

In those days there were no textbooks or 'how to' guides on healing and I had to learn about my powers through trial and error. Restoring people to health was evidence that my powers worked, but I wasn't satisfied with that. I had always been a logical person who liked to understand things, and it was the same when it came to dealing with my gift. I wanted to prove that what I did made scientific sense and I spent a lot of time searching for someone who could tell me that.

Eventually I found some scientists in Milan who ran all sorts of tests on me to see how strong my energy was. They found that I had the highest levels of power that they had seen at that stage.

These scientific tests were the external confirmation of my gift. I had known from the start that something incredible was happening inside me. I could feel that it was a truly physical phenomenon, one that seemed beyond my control, and my results with people were so rapid and dramatic that it was obvious that I was changing them at a deep cellular level. But with this information from Milan I had a clearer idea of what I was doing.

Decisions, Decisions...

When I arrived back home in Sarajevo from Milan I had to deal with even more attention than before. The media had a new slant on my story and this was too much for me to handle. I just wanted to get on with my life. I understood what I did much more clearly now and I wanted to focus on using my gift and to get away from the craziness around me.

Soon afterwards, I had to face some of the biggest decisions in my life. I was invited to set up a Bio-Energy clinic in the Canary Islands, where I could do more research into my healing powers. Even though it was a major step, I didn't think about this for long. Not speaking any language other than my mother tongue, I left home with only my son and a handful of possessions, leaving behind my country, my broken marriage, my family and my friends. I just knew that I had to go. It felt like the right thing to do and I didn't question it: if I had, I would never have gone. In fact, strangely for me, it was only when I was writing my first book and I was reading back over my life story that I realized how mad some of my decisions might seem to someone else. I even wondered myself how on earth I could have left like that without worrying about money, my child, the language barrier and my own security – but my decision always felt right.

It proved to be right too. Both my reputation and the clinic's built steadily and patients came from all over the world – mainland Spain, Italy, Germany, the UK and even as far afield as America. After a few years there, I was invited to set up a clinic in the UK. I could picture myself in a clinic in London where everything was set up properly and I also saw myself dealing with the media – and, as before, I just knew it was the right thing to do. I didn't question my gut feeling – I just left.

Within two months of being in London I had my own clinic in Hampstead, just as I had imagined. At the time, ME (myalgic encephalopathy, or chronic fatigue syndrome) was a big health issue that the medical community was struggling to understand, but it was an area in which I got great results. I had worked with a woman who had recovered so well that the media pounced on the story. Before I knew it I found myself on radio and TV shows – and with only about 100 words of English in my vocabulary, that was quite some feat! After these appearances, the phone rang non-stop and soon I was extremely busy treating people, including many sportspeople and celebrities. It seemed that coming to London had been the right move.

As you can see, this part of my story ends on a high, but over the years I have had as many downs as ups. I know that some people thought I was mad to leave Sarajevo and then again to leave the Canaries, but I think that the way my life has developed has proved that following my instinct was the right thing to do. I look back now and see that everything has happened for a reason. In fact nothing happens through coincidence – we create everything in our lives. In my own life I have never crumbled in times of stress, I have always just got on with whatever I needed to sort out. I don't know if I was born like that, but I do know that it's through dealing with the challenges and coming out the other side of them in a better place that I have come to the point of writing this book.

Everybody has their fair share of ups and downs, and so I'm sure that each of you will be aware that you may not notice at the time how everything is going to fall into place, but looking back, you can see that certain steps in your life were meant to happen.

All of us can gain a huge amount from learning about how energy is affecting us all the time – not just when we are ill, but at every step and turning point. By becoming aware of and controlling what we SEND out and what we RECEIVE, we can affect what we think, how we feel and what we attract.

CHAPTER 2

The Energy Pyramid

Whilst this book is designed to be a practical guide to help you improve your connection to your energy and attract what you want in life, I'd like first of all to explain more fully what I mean when I use the word 'energy'. This will make it easier for you to understand what is to come.

When I explain something, I often find it best to look at the big picture and then drill down into the detail, and the same goes for energy. I'd like to make clear at this point that this is not a definitive text on energy. Energy is a huge subject and one you could study for the rest of your life; this book covers what I think is important for you to know to get what you want.

Everything in the world – people, objects, places, animals, plants, water, thoughts and emotions – has its own frequency and therefore own energy field. Some people refer to this electromagnetic frequency as *chi*, *prana*, *ki* or 'life force', but I simply call it 'energy'.

There are four main dimensions of energy, which I like to think of as being like a pyramid. Despite the different levels of

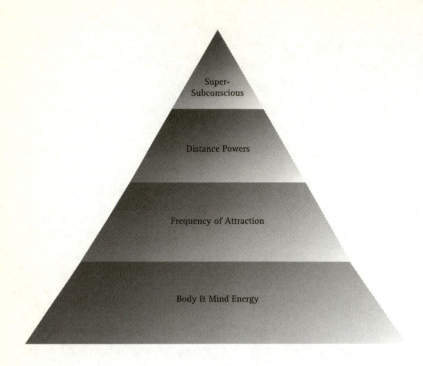

the pyramid, the energy is the same, it just manifests in different ways. Just as ice, water and steam are all different forms of the same compound (H_2O), these four levels are different ways in which you can experience energy.

The Super-Subconscious

This is where all information since the beginning of time is stored. It is also known as universal energy. Billions of years of memories, facts and experiences exist at this level, which is a bit like a central library. Everything you could ever need to know is already here; you just have to know how to connect to it.

Super-Subconscious energy is affected by planetary influences such as the phases of the moon and tidal patterns. The way in which you interact with this energy comes down to how well you can tap into it. You can 'click in' or 'click out' of it and I'll be showing you how to do that.

An analogy that works particularly well here is that of satellites. We rely on satellites for a number of things, including watching television, making calls on a mobile phone, getting weather reports and finding our way around using GPS (global position systems or satnavs). The satellites are always there, but we only connect to them when we want to use their ability to communicate. Hence, we click in or click out.

Similarly, you can click in or click out of contact with the Super-Subconscious. Devices that communicate with a satellite have an antenna to do this, and you have your own kind of antenna that picks up the energy that you decide to attract. So you can SEND and RECEIVE communications in a similar way to machines connecting with satellites orbiting the Earth.

Distance Powers

This is where we find mass energy forces such as distance healing powers. Just as the Super-Subconscious can be compared to satellite communication, so this level of energy can be compared to mobile phone communication. Every one of us communicates in this way, whether or not we are aware of it. We can connect to one person like this or have conference calls with more than one person, and so we often experience this level of energy when we are in a large group of people that is being influenced in a similar way. 'Crowd mentality' like this happens at demonstrations or concerts, through the energetic force of the media and political messages, and other cultural and social milieux.

I find that it can help to think of this energy in a visual way by drawing a parallel with the animal world: when fish swim together as a school, when ants combine forces to undertake mammoth tasks or when geese fly in formation, each group combines its energy to be greater than the individual parts.

In our case, when many human minds come together at the same energetic frequency, they act like one mind and become more powerful than the individual mind of each person. When this energy exists, it can seem as if large groups of people are acting like sheep, unable to think for themselves and easily influenced by energies more powerful than their own. This can be a positive force (for example creating an electric atmosphere at a concert or carnival) but also a negative, draining one. One example is the power of mass fear. Fear is the most powerful energetic frequency and I'll be showing you how you can protect yourself from it. Another example is the energy surrounding the credit crunch – something that is particularly poignant right now.

The important thing for you to know is that you play a critical part in creating mass energy both by SENDING it and by allowing yourself to RECEIVE it and be influenced by it – whether consciously or not.

The Frequency of Attraction

Have you ever met someone and felt an instant connection with them that you just can't explain? This isn't necessarily because of physical or sexual attraction, it's just that you're on the same wavelength and something between you clicks. Each and every thing and person in the universe has its own energetic pull and that's what you feel when you connect with someone like this – your personal energy frequency finds another one that matches or complements it.

This 'frequency of attraction' is created not only between individual people but also between groups of people with whom you share a relationship, such as your family, friends or colleagues, so there are webs of energy fields all around you. These also exist between you and objects that are an extension of your energy. You'll see this idea in practice when we come on to look at how to find things you've lost. I call this the 'frequency of attraction' because it is an intimate level of communication and it relates to what you bring into your life.

We all have many personal experiences of RECEIVING messages from people. Often by simply thinking about someone we can in the same second get a text message, phone call or email from them. This type of experience is familiar to everyone and I'm sure you can think straightaway of times when something like this has happened to you. They are not just 'coincidences'. As with the energetic exchanges that happen at the other levels of energy in the pyramid, when you think about a particular person, you actually SEND out a message to them. If they are in tune with their own energy, as well as yours, they will RECEIVE that message on an energetic level. Though they may not consciously be aware of what is happening, they may find themselves deciding to call, email or even visit you. The idea might just pop into their head and they won't know why.

Body and Mind Energy

When I'm healing, I work with this frequency of energy. I RECEIVE information about people as soon as they come near me, sometimes even before I put my hands on them. I connect with every part of a person's body and wherever there is a block, I feel their pain. This is because I am adjusting their frequency back to its healthy level, which their body holds in its memory.

I RECEIVE whatever information I get without analyzing or judging it. I also 'listen' more to what I pick up from people's

energy than I do from their words. It's a bit like reading a book –
I get a picture of someone's problem by picking up the disturbed
frequency.

> *A lady came to see me a few weeks ago and told me, 'There's
> nothing wrong with me. I've just come to see you for a boost.' As
> soon as I started treating her I knew that there was something
> wrong with her left lung. I found a way to mention it to her and
> she said, 'Oh yes, I know I've got a problem there.' She just had
> chosen not to mention it.*
>
> *I don't always say anything to people about their medical
> conditions, as it may not be appropriate or necessary, but at
> other times it's important to acknowledge what they've been
> through or the health problems they have.*

I can't help but RECEIVE information when I work, but you
will probably find that it's much easier to have this kind of energetic communication with someone you know well or to whom
you are close, as you will already share a frequency with them.
This doesn't mean you can always read each other's minds or
know exactly what someone else is thinking all of the time, but
unconsciously you will be able to SEND and RECEIVE messages
much more easily when you are aware of other people's energetic
frequency. This is how psychic ability works.

It may help to think of *all* of these kinds of connections and communications in terms of radio frequencies. You cannot see radio
frequencies, and if the radio is off you can't hear them, but you
know that each station is still putting out signals and that the
people who have tuned in are RECEIVING them. If you think of
energetic frequencies in the same way, it is easier to understand
how other people affect you.

Given the things I have experienced first hand, as well as the experiences that other people have told me about, I find it interesting that many people don't believe in the power of the mind and/or energy. Scientists admit that the mind is more powerful than a computer and that we still only understand a tiny percentage of what it can do, yet those who are cynical about energy like to pass off experiences where we connect with others as 'chance' or 'coincidence'. Hopefully, by reading this book, you will be able to understand and make more of these magical experiences in your own life.

CHAPTER 3

The Power of Neutral Mind

When you were reading about the challenges and struggles I've had to overcome throughout my life, you may have noticed that I often acted on my instinct and made decisions quickly. In order to do this, I had to be in a state of NEUTRALITY, and this is key to being able to tap into the energy frequencies around you, so I'm now going to explain it fully to you.

What Is Neutral Mind?

NEUTRAL MIND is a space where you don't analyze or judge, you are simply present to what you're doing. You have heightened sensitivity and so you can access the Super-Subconscious. Buddhists call this way of being 'non-attachment' and some people refer to it as 'being in the now'.

In this state you are also observant, and when you are observant, you step back from a situation, which makes it easier for you to control your reaction to it and, therefore, your energy. When you are aware of what is around you and the effect it is having on you, you can calibrate your energy and be confident about how people, places, situations and things are affecting you.

This state of NEUTRAL MIND is a powerful state of balance in which you vibrate at your correct, healthy frequency, and magic happens when you're in this place: you make the right decisions and get what you want and you also find yourself not being affected by negative things that would otherwise upset you.

Other times when you could have NEUTRAL MIND are situations when your survival instinct kicks in; for example you may have heard stories of people harnessing supernatural strength at times when they really have to, and it's usually when their or someone else's life is in danger. This can also sometimes happen when you are lost, for example in a wooded area or at sea, with no sense of where you are; lost in your car without a sense of direction; 'lost' because of your emotions, or because you're ill and fighting for your life. At times like these, when nobody else can help you, if you find NEUTRALITY without questioning what you're doing, your instinct takes over and your mind opens up. You don't usually have time to judge or analyze what's going on – instead you find incredible strength and just seem to know what to do, as this woman's story shows.

> One winter's day I was walking in a remote part of the mountains. The weather was very snowy and cold and I had been walking for hours. I had no idea where I was, only that I was a good few hours away from civilization.
>
> Suddenly, I started to get pain in my chest. I don't know if the cold was getting to me, but I started to panic. My legs were like jelly, my heart was pounding and I was finding it hard to breathe. I had no idea whether to carry on and fight or give up and face goodness knows what. It was getting dark and I had to make a decision. I decided to carry on.

I walked without thinking. I just put one foot in front of the other. Somehow my pain seemed to disappear and I don't know how I did it, but two hours later I reached a house. I didn't think about who might be inside, I just knocked on the door and, luckily, found help.

This woman had no idea how strong she could be, but she found an enormous emergency reserve from somewhere. She had to survive and if she'd stopped for one moment to contemplate the pros and cons of carrying on, she probably would never have taken the risk. But she went with what came to her and, luckily, she was fine. This was the NEUTRAL MIND at work. By being in this state, she found that the right answer and the strength to do the right thing came to her when she needed them most.

When you are in NEUTRAL MIND, not only do you act without analyzing but you are also emotionally detached and this helps you to see the big picture and make the right decisions.

It can be easy to get confused about the idea of emotional detachment, especially when it comes to situations that involve people who are close to you. For example, if you are a parent and your child is ill, you can care about them by stepping back from the situation and the emotions, and observing what is going on. By not being emotionally involved you can see the real picture so you won't get caught up in thinking about the worst-case scenario. From the standpoint of NEUTRAL MIND, you won't pass on to anyone any negative energy you may be feeling, such as fear or panic.

Neutral Mind – You Know More Than You Think

To be able to make the most of this powerful state, you need to be able to recognize when you're in it. Just as you SEND and

RECEIVE energetic messages without consciously doing so, you are often in a state of NEUTRAL MIND without realizing it. It isn't something new that you have to learn, you just have to learn to *recognize* it, because you have been experiencing it since you were born.

We are all born into this world to be ultimately happy, healthy and get the best out of ourselves. In the early stage of life our senses are at their strongest and we are more open to new development and absorbing knowledge. This is the time when we are in our purest state of NEUTRALITY. However, it is also at this stage that we are much more open to outside suggestive influences.

From the moment we start to be conditioned by knowledge from the outside world, we start to slowly lose the connection we have with our natural instincts and our own intuition. In the diagram on page 24, we can see how the NEUTRAL MIND of an adult loses connection with the super-subconscious in comparison to a child.

As we grow and develop, we open ourselves up to the influences and exposure of life. We are conditioned by our environment, society, class, education, religion, family and the social groups around us. Whether positive or negative, these external influences (or man-made boxes) begin to shape who we are and how we think. Only when we see beyond these boxes and constraints within everyday life can we recognize who we are and what we essentially need.

It is often the case that it is only when people become ill or find themselves in a negative relationship or badly suited career path, that they become aware of their need to reconnect with their natural self and own gravitational pulls within life. Sometimes important decisions in life, such as choosing a partner or taking on a certain job, are made due to other pressures or people around us, rather than by listening and paying attention to our natural instincts. If we were all more in tune with our natural energy frequencies and instincts, the way children are, we would be more likely to use our NEUTRAL MIND to make healthier and happier choices.

By recognizing and encouraging this natural skill that we each have to use and trust our own instincts, I believe we could all achieve much more out of life. Hopefully in the future this type of learning will be instilled in schools and taught at an early age, in order to protect and nurture the NEUTRAL MIND and the hidden powers we all have. In today's modern world, children have to deal with so many more 'unnatural' influences, like computers, mobile phones and the internet. Although these new technologies are all made to aid our lives and understanding, they also contribute to limiting our minds and the extent to which we use the natural abilities with which we are born.

As you will start to notice, NEUTRAL MIND comes to us when we are happy and unstifled by thoughts and pressures. To access NEUTRAL MIND you need to pay attention to the following:

- Remember what you feel like when you are doing something that relaxes you and makes you feel balanced.

- Acknowledge that this is a feeling that you get in your whole body and mind. This can feel a bit like the blissful state you are in just before you fall asleep.

- Recognize an overwhelming sense of knowing that you are in the right place.

- Be aware of how you feel when you are doing things you really need to do.

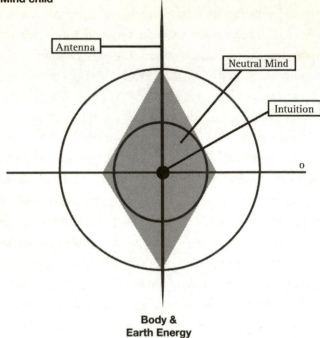

A) Neutral Mind child

Super-Subconscious

Antenna

Neutral Mind

Intuition

o

Body &
Earth Energy

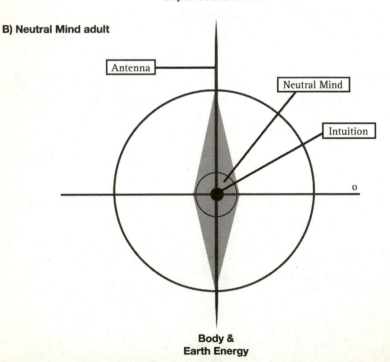

Super-Subconscious

B) Neutral Mind adult

Antenna

Neutral Mind

Intuition

o

Body &
Earth Energy

We have all experienced situations where we have acted upon our instinct, even when it went against other advice and information, and this is one of the best things you can focus on to access NEUTRAL MIND.

Neutrality in Practice

So, what does this all mean in practice? What kinds of things do you do as an adult that put you in a NEUTRAL state?

When I'm healing, I'm in a NEUTRAL state. When I'm at home I go about my life just like any other person: I shop, make dinner, spend time with my family and friends, talk about what happened during the day, watch a little television, read to relax, and so on. But the minute I open the door to my clinic, I put to one side all of the other details of my life. I become totally present to my patients and I observe what is going on for them. By being open to receiving information, I can recognize their frequency and transform it, move it to where it needs to be. By learning to be in NEUTRALITY, I have been able to work intensely and con-sistently for nearly 30 years. NEUTRALITY has protected me from emotional attachment with my patients – and also benefitted them by making them heal more quickly and with better results.

All of us are different and so find NEUTRALITY in different ways. But regardless of how we do it, we all relax and enter a state similar to meditation. This can come about through activi-ties like swimming, walking, painting, drawing, cooking, running – and, of course, meditating. Some people who perform on stage, such as actors, singers, musicians and comedians, go into NEU-TRAL MIND as soon as they get on a stage.

You can also find that some very successful business people switch into NEUTRALITY to see the big picture of a commercial situation and to make the best decision. Athletes who want to reach the top of their sport enter NEUTRALITY to beat records and win medals; they call this the 'zone' and when they are in this place, everything feels effortless. If you have any special ability, gift or talent that feels natural to you and that you feel compelled to use, you are probably in NEUTRAL MIND when you are doing it.

Later on I'll be giving you some exercises that will help you practise getting into a NEUTRAL state, but first of all let's look at why NEUTRALITY is important for you.

Why Is Neutrality Important for You?

Protection

Life is full of hypnotic suggestions that work both on our body and mind and also affect our energy frequency. If you've ever seen a stage hypnotist in action, you will probably have seen tricks like someone willingly eating a raw onion or a lemon because they were given the suggestion that the food they were holding was an apple. But you don't have to be a trained hypnotist to SEND powerful messages like this – we RECEIVE (and SEND) messages that are this powerful every day. The thing to watch out for, however, is whether the information we take in is good for us.

If we get suggestions from people we trust, believe and respect, like our parents, teachers and doctors, they can be particularly powerful in a good or a bad way.

One of my patients had brain cancer and when I first met her, she had been given two months to live. Because her tumour was growing so large, it was starting to push one of her eyeballs out of her head and it was also causing her epileptic fits. After a week of sessions with me, her epilepsy had stopped and her tumour was smaller. Her eye was sitting properly in her eye socket again. She was so happy and full of hope that she and her boyfriend decided to get married.

A few weeks later she went to her doctor to tell him the good news. She returned to my clinic the next day in floods of tears. She had told her doctor how good she was feeling and showed him her eye. She had also told him that she was not having any epileptic fits. The doctor had replied, 'Tell your future husband to take the next two months off work, because in my opinion you won't be alive after that.'

I couldn't believe he'd said this and couldn't understand how he could think that it would be at all helpful. Luckily for this woman, she refused to latch on to his negativity, shook off what he had said and focused on getting better. I'm happy to report that a year on she is now happily married – and about to have a baby. Her tumour has completely disappeared. She has proved her doctor wrong, which has been fantastic for her, her husband and their future child.

This story is one the most inspiring examples of why a NEU-TRAL state is important. After the initial shock and upset, this woman didn't allow herself to be affected by what her doctor said. She didn't despair and panic, as some people would have done. She was feeling so good and had such great evidence that she was getting better that she turned her mind away from the idea of dying and focused instead on living.

To stay NEUTRAL, you have to learn to listen to what you hear *without* letting yourself be affected. You need to act as an observer – and if you hear or see a message that is negative, you need to stop yourself tapping into the energy of it. You could say that you need to let things go, 'like water off a duck's back'.

Problem-Solving

As well as being NEUTRAL when you're dealing with your own problems, it's vital that you stay that way when you are helping other people. Some people think that when things go wrong they should sympathize with the person who's suffering. But by adopting an attitude of 'Poor you!' you actually can't help anyone, especially if it's a friend or a relative. Whilst it may seem that you're being nice if you sympathize, you can't help someone shift into NEUTRALITY by doing that. You need to help them change their energy:

- Encourage them to see the good that they can take out of a situation.

- Help them to move on. What can they focus on to leave behind whatever has upset them?

- Don't let them be a victim – and don't be one yourself either.

- Help them work out how they can change the situation.

There have been times when I've had a problem that I've only been able to solve by being in a NEUTRAL state. Several years ago, when I was trying to move house, I thought I had found the perfect place but then realized I couldn't afford it. I was so disappointed because I'd already got attached to the house and had put my energy into it, even before it was definitely mine. By doing this and being emotionally attached, I had shifted from my place of NEUTRALITY and was left really upset when my offer was rejected.

What's interesting is that I vividly remember the moment when the problem sorted itself out. I was out running on the beach with my husband and I started to see all the positive reasons why we hadn't bought that house, like the fact that it didn't have the view that I really wanted. I started to feel that there would be something better for us. By seeing the reasons why that property wasn't right for us, I felt really good and I let go of it. I shifted to being NEUTRAL about it.

Literally a few minutes later, I saw a house for sale. It looked amazing and straightaway we decided to see it. When we viewed it, it was perfect – but it was also a little out of our league. But rather than just setting my heart on it, this time I knew something felt right and, as if by magic, my husband got some extra work just in time for us to be able to buy it.

The minute I let go of what was holding me back, something better came into my life in a split second – and that house is where we live today.

As it turned out, a friend of mine could afford the first house I'd seen and it was right for him. He bought it and so everything turned out for the best for everyone. My friend and I both got the right homes and I can visit his house any time I want!

Disasters and misfortune can be good for you as they can make you recognize what is right and what is wrong for you. At times like these you need to stop and ask yourself, what is the silver lining in all this? You have to talk it through with someone, look at the reasons why what happened is for the best. Why was it meant to happen? What were the bad things about what you wanted? In the future you'll be able to look back and see how things have turned out for the best, but the key is seeing it *now*. It may not look good at the moment, but you need to bring your ability to rationalize forward to the present, where it can make the most difference.

Decision-Making

We are all faced with decisions all the time, so it's really important that we find a way to make good decisions. When you question something, you will always find a reason not to do it – a reason why it's not sensible, why it's not the right time or why it's safer to stay as you are. But when you make a decision without questioning then you know that your intuition is guiding you and it must be right. All the major decisions that I've taken in my life have been based on my gut feeling. When I left my native country to move to the Canary Islands and then when I moved from the Canaries to the UK, I left within days of deciding. I just knew that what I was doing was right. I've come to learn to be NEUTRAL and not to analyze a situation.

You too have to recognize this state and trust it, and in my experience if you do this, things always work out. We can rationalize a situation until we're blue in the face, but deep down we know what's best for us – we just feel it. Each and every one of us has an instinct that tells us when something sits well with us and when it doesn't. It may sound obvious, but when you make the right intuitive choices, you feel good – you literally buzz or vibrate at the right level – and when your body and mind are in balance, your intuition opens up.

When you make a poor choice, you feel it too. It may be a sinking feeling or a lump in your stomach, perhaps you can't sleep at night or you have no appetite, or maybe you have a recurring injury or physical condition. By moving from your natural frequency, you leave yourself open to niggles and disease, and when you're in an unhealthy state, you make unhealthy decisions.

Think back to a time when you didn't listen to your gut instinct, a time when you sensed that you should make one choice but you did something else. What happened as a result? Often in these cases, you may have ended up missing a train, taking the wrong job or getting stuck in a draining relationship. Looking back to situations like these, you can probably see that you knew deep down that your choice was wrong, but you went with it anyway.

On the flip side, when you find something you really need in your life, there is no struggle. When you meet the right partner or friend, things just seem to come together, even against the odds. If the perfect job comes along, it feels right and you find yourself not wanting to question it. And when you walk into your future home, your energy starts to feel positive and strong. It can sometimes be scary to go with the flow of your intuition, but chances are it's the best thing.

NEUTRALITY is a state of mind that opens the door to our intuition. Many things, like stress, illness and fear, can stop us from accessing our NEUTRAL MIND, yet ironically these things often also spur us on to find NEUTRAL MIND when there is no other help or explanation at hand.

One of the times when I often see people naturally switching to NEUTRALITY in their decision-making is when they are at their lowest point. They might have lost a loved one, all their money or their hope. In these moments, the most important decisions you can make are:

- To let go of what you no longer want in your life by focusing on something else.

- Not to focus on what you don't want.

- To pull yourself up from your low point.

- To make the brave decision to lift yourself into the light and into your future.

How to Nurture Your NEUTRAL MIND

One of the key things you can do to find NEUTRALITY is to go with your instinct and hunches and not ignore the energetic messages you RECEIVE. By recognizing these instances and following them over and over again, you will start to become more in control of what you RECEIVE and, in turn, what you SEND out.

> *A while ago I needed to go to hospital for an appointment. As I was waiting for the bus I saw a lady across the road come out of her house and get into her car. At that moment, I thought to myself, 'Wouldn't it be lovely if she was going into town and gave me a lift?' The next thing I knew, she wound down her window and asked if I was going far and whether she could give me a lift. I was shocked! It was as if she had read my mind.*

Coincidence is more than just a chance event. You should look at anything that seems to happen to you 'by chance' and consider:

- Why did you RECEIVE a particular message or energy?

- Who or where did it come from?

- Why did it come to you at that time?

- Why were you open to receiving it?

- When did you let yourself open up to recognizing the gut feelings that guided you to the best choice?

- What led up to that happening?

When you gather this information, you will have perfect examples of when you are using your NEUTRALITY.

There are also other things you can do to help nurture your NEUTRAL MIND – and you might just be surprised at how simple they are.

1. Be aware of your thoughts

Recognizing and acknowledging what's in your mind puts you a long way towards being NEUTRAL, because as soon as you make this acknowledgement, you start to be in control of your body, mind, soul and instinct. You also start to reprogram your mind.

Everyone can start this process, even if not everyone can put into words how they're feeling, in my experience. But it's not about words – it's about the feelings you have and the things you do.

> One of my patients said to me, 'I have nothing to live for, nothing to look forward to.' She was in her early thirties and had a child and a lovely home – all she was missing was the right partner.
>
> I asked her what she wanted. What kind of person would she like to share her bed and home? What did she love doing? But she couldn't answer me. Her head was so full of what she didn't have that she had no space or energy to spend on looking forward to life.

No matter how bad you feel you can always:

- Think ahead to what you want.

- Change your thoughts and focus on CANCELLING the negative thoughts that you're used to thinking.

When you do this, you control your negative programming and access your NEUTRAL state. Hopefully, when you start to see how much this state will help you, you will take the steps you need to work on yourself. And once you can recognize what your mind is doing and what's blocking you from getting what you want, you've already started the process of attracting what you would like to have in your life.

2. Focus outwards, not inwards

Lots of people spend so much time in their own head that they don't even notice what's around them. To experience NEUTRAL MIND, you need to feel a part of your surroundings and connect to them. You may have heard the famous phrase 'Smell the roses'? Well, there is a great deal of truth in this. Here are some ideas on how to go about it:

- Step out into nature and feel a part of the living things around you.

- Enjoy the colours of flowers in the park or in your garden.

- Watch the birds flying past.

- Go to places where you can be surrounded by greenery.

- Spend time near water and listen to the sound of it.

- Take in the elements of life, such as the wind and the earth, that are removed from our built-up world.

- Be aware of the sky and notice the shape and formation of clouds.

- Observe the stars and the moon at night and be part of their energy.

Looking outwards helps you to take your attention away from any negative thoughts in your head and change your focus to things that are natural and positive. You need to recognize that, although only a tiny part of it, you *are* a part of the universe, and so are connected to everything around you.

This is a form of 'active' meditation and there are other ways in which you can choose to relax in a similar way. Everybody can find their own way to relax and clear their mind. It doesn't matter what suits you, as long as it works. You can sit cross-legged in silence. You can listen to music. You can use a mantra. As long as it works, do it!

3. Express yourself

I'm a great advocate of self-expression and this helps us all relax and be in a Zen-like state. You can express your creativity in many ways: through reading, writing, cooking, flower arranging, gardening, embroidery, sewing, knitting, decorating, tinkering with cars, sculpting, singing or painting – basically through any hobby that you enjoy.

I find that painting helps me to relax and find a zone where I can open up to the Super-Subconscious. My ideas come from a place deep inside me and I channel what I feel in the moment. I just follow this energy with my movements onto the canvas and then start to recognize what I'm painting.

4. Watch your language

Every single word has its own frequency, partly because of the meaning we attach to it. 'Good' has a different frequency from 'bad', and 'hate' carries a different energy from 'love'. We feel the energy of these words when we hear, read and say them. Because of this, the language you use is critical to NEUTRAL MIND.

It's interesting, too, that meaning can sometimes be irrelevant to the energy we feel from words. If someone spoke to you in a language that you didn't understand, you would still be able to pick up on the energy of what they were saying.

You may have seen the way hypnotists work with people, telling them what to do or think, but the most powerful suggestions you can give your mind come from yourself! You are your own hypnotist and the things you say to yourself have a direct impact on how you behave and what you believe.

Later on you'll get a chance to practise using the power of words to give yourself positive energy, but for now just look at the words below and notice how they make you feel.

FLOW   CREATIVITY
     ENERGY
LOVE   CUDDLES
     STRENGTH
  PEACE   SKY
              CALM
   FLOWERS
              WARMTH
ENERGY NATURE   FUN
              SMILE
  COMPASSION
              FRAGRANCE
PASSION   MELODY
   JOY   LAUGHTER
       GIGGLE
  COMFORT   GRASS
          BEAUTY
KINDNESS BABY   HAPPINESS

  MELODY   HEALTH
              GOODNESS
OCEAN WARMTH
              LOVE
          KISS
PLEASURE   SUNSHINE

5. Respect yourself

There are certain other things about the way in which we treat ourselves that affect whether or not we are in a NEUTRAL state. For example, most people look and feel better – and so their energy feels better – when they take care of their appearance by making themselves look nice with clothes, make-up, and so on. You don't have to wear expensive fancy clothes, you just need to show that you care for and respect yourself enough to make an effort. It may be wearing a suit and tie, perfume or lipstick, or doing your hair. People who take more pride in themselves often tend to have better health too; it's important for them to feel good and look after their body on the inside and outside.

Some other ways of showing yourself respect include:

- Eating well.

- Being active.

- Limiting alcohol consumption.

- Keeping your home neat, tidy and clean. (If your home or office is a mess, it will affect your energy. Many people who live in a mess are depressed. It's very common to see the two things go hand in hand, because clutter and depression share a similar energetic frequency.)

Your outside world mirrors your inside world and, even if you haven't noticed it before, you can start putting yourself on the right track to NEUTRAL MIND by sorting out the places where you spend your time. The practice of *feng shui* is based on the belief that our environment affects our energy, and people find that by following its principles, their home can feel completely different and more energized. Trust me that when you do this, you will feel better and freer, and when you make space in your environment, new things will come into your life.

You can also lift your energy by doing other things that you enjoy, like listening to a particular piece of music, dancing to your favourite song or eating your favourite food. We all have things that boost our energy and make us feel motivated and positive.

Experts in Neutrality

Animals are naturally in a NEUTRAL state and have an intuitive ability to sense and act on energy frequencies around them. For example, you may notice your pets acting strangely if the weather is about to change, if an earthquake is about to happen, if anything is wrong with you or if they can sense danger in any way. Animals act on their energetic senses without analyzing what they're feeling. When I do distance healing, people often report to me that their pets get drawn to the energy and snuggle up next to them during the session.

This next story shows how straightforward it is to heal animals because of their natural NEUTRALITY:

A couple of years ago my best horse and advanced eventer, Billy, suffered an injury to his hoof that meant that he was in extreme pain and unable to walk. After veterinary treatment and four months of rest, he was still incredibly lame. I took him up to see some of the best vets in the country, but even they didn't know what to do. After an MRI scan, they concluded that the one side of the foot had lost all blood circulation and that the bruising and tear were very deep. They were pessimistic about his future and said he might well never compete again. I brought him home with very little hope.

As a last resort, I thought I'd give Seka a call to see if there was anything she could do. She asked for a picture of Billy and did distance healing on him every day for a week.

A couple of weeks later, he was able to trot. I was shocked – but I also didn't want us to get ahead of ourselves, so I left it another month, thinking it might just be a fluke. A month later Billy was absolutely fine. It really had worked!

We began work again slowly and within three months Billy was competing again. Six months after the vets had said he would probably not compete again, we were selected for a British team to take part in the European Championships in Hungary.

We have the same ability as animals to pick up on energetic frequencies, but because we also have the 'gift' of being able to think rationally, we often override our natural senses with thoughts and emotions. If we were all as NEUTRAL as animals, we'd have the most profound experiences in all areas of our life.

The time of our life when we are naturally most NEUTRAL is when we are very young, and that's why I also have great success treating babies and children. They are simple to treat because they don't have any other issues to get in the way of their treatment. Adults can be distracted by stress and other mental barriers when they're ill, and so I often have to help them overcome these issues before I can get to work on their physical illness, but with children, I can work directly with the condition.

A couple of years ago, I was treating a very poorly little baby. She was only two months old and she had many problems with her health, including a hole in her heart. Her conditions were affecting her sleep and she was crying a lot. Her parents were beside themselves and didn't know what to do to help her.

When she first came to my clinic, her cries were so shrill that they pierced the entire building. Everyone in the waiting room and on the other floors was distressed by the noise. She was so tiny that when I put my hands on her, they almost covered her – but the minute I did this, she stopped crying. Then she looked up at me as if to say, 'Ooh ... this feels nice.'

After she had been treated, she started sleeping and eating properly, and so she started growing. The hole in her heart closed up and she never cried again when she came to see me – instead she was always smiling. She loved her treatments and she knew when she saw me what was going to happen.

This little girl went from being really ill to making a wonderful recovery. She had no idea what was going on, so she didn't block my energy by judging, analyzing or worrying – all she knew was that it felt good when I was treating her.

The Challenge of Neutral Mind

As you'll see from all of the things you can do to nurture your NEUTRALITY, it is *simple* in theory but not necessarily *easy*. You need to respect your body, take time for yourself – and apply yourself.

For example, you might say to yourself, 'I want to run a marathon,' and, in theory, it's simple to run a marathon. You just have to train and train and keep running a bit further each day. You also have to eat and rest well. So the answer is *simple* – but it's not *easy*, because it requires you to do something every day.

To really use your NEUTRALITY in your life, you need to make an effort to know yourself inside and out. This is a natural way of being, but few people do it. It won't help you to look for a 'quick fix' for the things you're not happy with or to turn to someone else in the hope that they'll tell you what you should do: you know yourself better than anybody else and so *you're* the best person to make the decisions in *your* life.

CHAPTER 4

One Energy, One Mind

I now want to look at the energetic communication that happens at the level of distance powers – and one of the most powerful energetic influences at this level is that of mass energy.

As I have already written, as we grow up and learn about life we are given lots of information, and with this, we start to create our world – our thoughts, opinions, beliefs and experiences – and these shape who we become. These are things that we also experience on an energetic level and they take us away from our NEUTRALITY.

Lucky Number 13

A simple example of this is the belief in many Western countries about the number 13 and Friday 13th. Why do we believe these things are unlucky? Well, it's because we're told they're unlucky and then stories of bad luck related to them get passed on, and the media focuses on them and reinforces the idea. As a result, we take in the suggestion and let it affect us and more accidents happen on Friday 13th than on other days.

On the other hand, for some cultures, 13 is a lucky number. For example in the Sikh culture and in Italy, this number carries good luck. The same applies in my country and 13 has always been a lucky number for me. It was the number of my school, which I loved, and both when I left my country to move to the Canaries and when I left there to come to the UK, I moved on the thirteenth day of the month; these turned out to be the right decisions for me. Maybe if I'd been superstitious, these moves would never have happened.

We all have a choice about whether or not to be affected by common suggestions or superstitions. In this case, for example, we can see 13 as a 'good' number, a 'bad' number – or just a number that's neither positive nor negative.

You experience suggestions like this at both a conscious and an energetic level all the time, and so you already know about the effect that mass energy can have on you. It can be very powerful and you may not even be aware of what is happening. However, you need to be able to recognize these forces so you can make a choice about whether or not to engage with them – and also learn how to turn the negative ones to positives so that they will work in your favour.

One of the strongest mass energy influences that will be familiar for you is that of the media.

The Influence of the Media

Here are three very well-known incidents that show how the media can influence us in different ways.

In 2006, the television presenter Richard Hammond had a terrible car crash during filming in which he nearly died. The whole of Britain was shocked. Because Hammond was such a popular character, the entire country wanted him to get better. The vibe from the media coverage was also positive and the energy created from it carried people along to will him to get better. It was as if everyone was on his side and helped him recover.

In comparison to the positive healing energy that was created for Richard Hammond, in 2008 reality TV star Jade Goody was diagnosed with cervical cancer. Right from the start the energy was one of death, and this got stronger as the media campaign followed her decline. The public got swept along by this and it didn't help Jade to get better because people were suffering along with her rather than helping her and everyone who followed her story expected her to die.

I recognized the wrong direction of the media campaign that she had in part created and emailed her PR company, offering to try to help her, but they never replied. It seemed she had given up, because the media was carrying a story of sympathy, and I believe she passed away too quickly.

Another example of the power of the media and mass energy was the reporting of the death of Diana, Princess of Wales. Even some people from other countries who were not aware of either her or the British Royal Family were affected by the wave of mourning that swept over the world. People were engaged at an energetic level and many spoke of a 'feeling' or an 'energy' that seemed to take them over. Even people who didn't consciously want to get upset were drawn in by the energy because it was like a tidal wave created by the mass media that swept up anyone in its path.

Diana's energy had been powerful for years because of all the images, footage and endless newspaper articles about her. A lot of people loved her and she had been in the national aware-

ness for a long time and a part of people's lives, even those who never met her, because the media followed everything she did. When she died, the loss people felt was because of an emptiness of energy and a pull from the mass of grief and sadness. This grew into something that nobody would have imagined, and even today, many years on, most people can still remember not only the event and the coverage of it, but also how it affected them. This demonstrates the effect of the media at its most powerful.

Whenever people are exposed to the same coverage of world events, the media have an easier job of influencing them. Rather than having to change the minds of many hundreds of thousands of individuals, when large groups of people come together at an energetic level, the media only have one 'mind' to influence. This is similar to the power you see when a shoal of fish swims together or a pack of animals hunts.

When you learn to observe and detach from these powerful energies, you can protect yourself and choose with which ones you engage, and you have to do this if you want to stay in NEUTRAL MIND.

How to Protect Yourself

Mass energy can be both positive and negative, and so, because it can be easy to get carried along by this kind of mass force, you need to recognize what is happening around you.

Be an Observer

The key factor in having a *choice* about the energy you RECEIVE and SEND is your ability to observe what is going on around you. When you are not emotionally involved, you can see the big picture: it's like looking down with a bird's eye view of what is happening. Your ability to stand back, observe and make a choice is key, because when you do this you can make better decisions.

If you don't know how to recognize energy that is being used to influence and potentially manipulate you, or how to protect yourself against it, you can find yourself getting caught up in an energy that isn't right for you. You can get swept along by everyone else and what they're thinking, and so are less likely to make up your own mind.

Here are some particularly poignant examples of this mass energy in action:

The Big Freeze

When we are affected by dramatic changes in the weather, we have to see them in a positive way. When snow hit the UK earlier this year (2010), we all had a choice as to how we reacted. The snow was already there and there was nothing we could do to make it go away, so we had to decide what kind of experience we wanted and which energy we were going to connect to.

There was no point in moaning about the weather, so we could just decide to make the most of it. A lot of people did this and went outside to play like little kids – sledging in the park, making snowmen, taking photos of the beautiful scenery and trudging through freshly fallen snow. Those who were out playing were all really happy and probably have great memories of the snow. It didn't have to be a negative experience – it could be fun!

Keep Swine Flu at a Distance

Every year there is a very real danger of flu and so it is something to take seriously, but you don't have to buy into the extreme fear. You can be aware of it and choose not to see yourself being ill.

You can see yourself being healthy instead. By doing this, you can keep your immunity strong. You should also stop looking for any symptoms that the media bombards at you. You have to reject these negative messages and tell yourself that you, and those close to you, will be OK. If you put your attention on being well, you will be.

The Credit Crunch

At the time of writing, one of the biggest talking points is the credit crunch. There's no doubt that this is a very real phenomenon in the world right now and we can't do anything about it. The only thing we can do is decide how we're going to get through it. The first things you need to do are:

- Decide not to be a part of it.

- See yourself staying afloat and surviving rather than sinking on the same ship as everyone else.

- Fill up the empty space with creativity, which could turn out to be to your advantage.

The best thing is to think about what you can do to make your life better. Maybe this means changing jobs, retraining, running your business in a different way or being creative about how you get work. Although it may not seem like the most obvious thing to do, you can see this period as an intriguing challenge for you – and even an opportunity to make a fresh start. Perhaps now you can do something you've always wanted to do. Make sure you see yourself doing well and succeeding at whatever you choose.

When challenging things happen, you have to use your survival instinct to get through them. This drive to survive puts you in a state of NEUTRALITY and then your mind will naturally find the best way to solve the problem. When you believe that you will always cope, you will. You just have to find the space in yourself to believe it.

The Positive Side of Mass Energy

Mass energy can also be a very *positive force*. Sporting events such as the Olympics or World Cup really help to lift a country and generate excitement about life.

I was in Sarajevo during the 1984 Winter Olympics so I have experienced first hand how amazing and energizing this kind of energy can be when it's on a large scale. I remember everybody being friendly and generous, both to their own countrymen and to foreign visitors, and taxi drivers sometimes didn't even charge their fare.

I'm really excited now about being in London for the 2012 Olympics and I think the whole of the UK will experience a lift in energy during the games. It will be an amazing time. When the announcement was made on 6 July 2005, the buzz in London was incredible, and this buzz will continue for the next few years. The nation will start to be proud and the energy around that event will be really positive and powerful. Each person will feel as though they're representing their country in their own way and the live events that are shown on television will be particularly powerful for us all. It's something we should really look forward to.

Other examples of the buzz of positive 'crowd mentality' can be seen at music concerts and other live entertainment events. The energy can feel almost drug-like in its ability to make you feel elated and lifted. You don't even have to be present at them: watching them on live television can be just as powerful. If you watch a sporting event in a pub with lots of fellow supporters or watch a charity event on live television at home, you can see how the positive force of energy can be used for a good outcome.

It's really important to join in with these things as they happen. If you record and then watch these kinds of events after they've actually taken place, you will have a different experience, as you won't be caught up in the energy of the moment.

Aside from large nation- or worldwide events, there are lovely things that happen every day on a smaller scale that you can choose to enjoy. For example, when the sun is shining and everyone heads to the park for picnics, games, fun and sunbathing, you can join in the energy of relaxation and happiness. By spending time with friends and family you love and who love you, you will also be able to feed off the positive network of energy. Also, you may find that you are attracted to do things in groups with people who enjoy the same things as you, such as sports clubs, hobby groups or fan clubs. When you share experiences with people who have the same passions and enjoy the same things as you, you share a frequency that can feel powerful and motivating – and this frequency is infectious.

You Always Have a Choice

You can always turn negative energy into positive. You just have to choose to disengage from the negative and focus on the positive things. For example, many people think it's too late for us to make any kind of positive impact on the state of the environment, believing that any change we make will be too little, too late. When the negative energy of complacency spreads, more people start to give up. But I believe we can make a difference, not only through what we do on an individual level but more powerfully by coming together at an energetic level to create a mass energy of happiness and positivity.

Charity telethons, for instance, successfully create an energy not only of awareness but also of gratitude for those of us who don't live with hardship, as well as certainty that we can make a difference. The mass energy that is created makes us all want to do something positive as a group of people who care. Imagine what we could do if we could get the world to believe that every gesture *does* make a difference.

CHAPTER 5

Extension Powers

You may think that your energy is just in your body and mind, but it extends into the things you use every day and the things you love. For example, your diary, wallet, jewellery, clothes, glasses, bags, photos and anything with your handwriting on are examples of things that are extensions of your energetic frequency. I am able to heal people wherever they are in the world by having their photographs, and this is because of the extension of their energy in the pictures. Even your car is an extension of your body and frequency, so when someone drives too close to you, you can feel threatened and get an uncomfortable feeling in your gut, because they are disturbing your energy. Similarly, if someone breaks into your home, they are effectively breaking into your energy. It's not surprising that you feel sick or shocked if you experience a break-in: it's as if your whole system has been violated – and it has. It affects your whole energy.

Many people notice the effect of the extension of their energy when they move home. When you move your things out of a place you have been living in, you start to feel less connected until it's empty, and then you feel completely detached from it. When it stops being your home, it stops being an extension of you. Then, as you move your things into a new house, this house starts to feel like 'you'. You feel more comfortable and at home there as it becomes an extension of your energy. Your family and friends will also start to sense your energy in it when they come to visit. You will create the same energy in each place you live, because regardless of the location, size or style of home, it is always an extension of you.

This can also apply to places other than our homes. For example, my clinic is an extension of my energy because I spend so much time there healing people and the whole place becomes energized. Patients even say that they feel better just sitting in the waiting room! But if I left my clinic and took my things with me, my energy would also leave and the rooms would not feel the same.

Seek and You Will Find

You extend your energy to your belongings in this way without even knowing you're doing it. Another thing you may not be aware of is that when you lose something, you can still be connected to it, so you should never CANCEL your connection to it. When you CANCEL your connection to something, it stops being yours and it's less likely to come back to you. So, rather than panic and be upset, the answer is to relax and stay calm, knowing that whatever it is will make its way back to you.

When I first started working on this book and talking to patients about what I was writing, I found that many people had stories to share about their own experiences. So many people were getting things back through what often seemed like coincidence and I'd like to share some of these examples with you.

This woman had two experiences on consecutive days that showed how she was able to stay connected to her things:

I was on my way to my appointment with Seka when I received a call from my daughter, who sounded very upset. Her car had been broken into during the night and almost everything inside had been stolen, including a pair of shoes that she had bought for my granddaughter – her first pair of shoes in fact. My daughter didn't care about any of the other things in her car and was just upset about her baby's shoes. I was upset for her and we both kept thinking about them. They were the only things we both really wanted her to get back.

The next day, my daughter rang me again and this time she was over the moon. Someone had come to her door carrying a lot of things that he'd found strewn around the road. The guys who'd broken into her car had abandoned the things they didn't want and in amongst them were my granddaughter's new shoes! They were almost the only things my daughter got back, but she didn't care. They were all she had really wanted.

Because the woman and her daughter had subconsciously stayed connected to the shoes and wanted so much to get them back, they came back to them. The two women were not consciously aware of doing this.

The day after this, the same lady had a similar experience:

I was on the way to see Seka and as I sat down on the train I noticed that I no longer had my wallet. As well as all my money, credit cards and so on, my return train ticket had been in there. At that moment in my head, I said, 'I can't lose it. It's just not possible because I can't be without it.' I didn't want to believe it had gone. I knew I had to get it back.

About 10 minutes later, a man came up to me. He had my wallet and ticket! He had found me by following the seat number on my ticket. I was so pleased to have everything back.

You can see here that the moment this woman said, 'I can't lose it,' she maintained the extension of her energy and so her wallet came back to her easily.

Here's an experience of mine that shows how powerful laughter can be as a way of maintaining your connection to your belongings:

I was on holiday with my best friend and we were having an amazing time. We'd spent the week having fun and laughing, and even as we were on our way to the airport we were still giggling away. When we got off the bus, though, I realized I didn't have my bag with me. I must have left it on the pavement. Because we were in such a hysterical mood, the two of us burst out laughing, not even thinking that I might have lost it.

A second later, my phone rang. A friend had found my bag on the pavement. What was interesting was that we had been out with this friend the previous night and he had complimented me on that bag. By chance, he'd been passing the bus station and when he saw my bag he'd recognized it straightaway. Knowing we were at the airport, he immediately jumped in a cab and brought it to us.

By laughing and seeing the amusing side of the story, my friend and I had stayed in a good mood. We hadn't been able to see that the bag was lost and so hadn't CANCELLED our connection to it. We just hadn't been analyzing anything. My bag had still been an extension of me and so, of all the people wandering around the island on that day, it was my friend who had been drawn to the extension of my energy.

Laughing is a really good way of staying in a NEUTRAL state when something goes wrong and/or you lose something. You obviously still have to take steps to get back what you're looking for, but by maintaining the extension of your energy, you're likely to attract someone who will be kind and helpful – and your things will come back to you.

You Are in Control

What you're probably becoming aware of is that you have a lot of control over whether or not you find things that you've lost or have had stolen. The key thing is to become *aware* of the moment when you are in a NEUTRAL state and how you feel in that moment. You need to recognize it so that you can choose to go back to it the next time you lose something. The more you become aware of that state, the more you will reprogram yourself to go to it.

Here is a story of a man who did the right thing without knowing what he was doing:

I was in a restaurant one evening and left my briefcase in the cloakroom, which is what I usually do. When I went to collect it at the end of the meal, it wasn't there. It had been stolen.

I was upset about the whole experience, but was most upset about not having my diary. I was thinking, 'I can't lose my diary. I have everything I need in there: contacts, dates, work notes, ideas – months and months of precious information.' Subconsciously, I knew I had to get it back.

The next day, there was a knock on my front door. It was a taxi driver who had found my diary abandoned on a bridge. He hadn't found anything else, just the diary. I couldn't believe my luck.

In this story, the moment when this man moved into NEU-TRALITY was when he said in his head, 'I can't lose my diary.' He didn't accept that it was gone. So subconsciously he didn't let go of it, though he didn't expect it to come back to him. He didn't CANCEL his frequency to it and so knew more than he realized about how to get it back.

When this patient was telling me this story, he said it reminded him of a verse from the Bible:

'Ask and it will be given to you; seek and you will find; knock and the door will be opened to you. For everyone who asks, receives; those who seek, find; and to those who knock, the door will be opened.' Matthew 7:7–8

Regardless of whether or not you believe in the Bible, these verses sum up really neatly the process you need to go through to recognize the moment you are in NEUTRALITY to get back anything you've lost. When you are in the right state of mind, anything can happen – and sometimes in unexpected ways. Things come back to people all the time – and this includes you – so you know more than you think because you're probably not aware of what you're doing. Subconsciously you don't CANCEL the extension of your energy because you know you can't lose the things that are important to you.

Are You a Loser or a Finder?

In the examples so far in this chapter, you have seen that as important as it is for the person who's lost something to stay connected to it and not CANCEL their energy, an equally important role is played by the person who finds it. 'Finders' are people who are inclined to come across misplaced and mislaid items and who have a natural responsibility to pick up things that are still 'alive' and connected to their owner's energy.

As with the friend who found my bag when I was on holiday, the people who find things are often attracted to the energetic frequency of an item because it is familiar to them. This may be because they know or are related to the owner or because in some way they feel connected to the owner's energy.

I was out one evening having a few drinks with a friend. We went to about four or five different bars and had a great night. I usually wear glasses, but when we went into the last bar of the night, because it was really hot, they steamed up and so I had to take them off. I put them in the top pocket of my shirt because I thought they'd be safest there.

When we left to go home, we spent ages trying to find a cab and ended up walking for about a mile. When we finally got one, I suddenly realized the glasses that I usually wore every day were gone. I thought, 'I can't do anything without my glasses. I must get them back.' I was panicking, but we were too far from the bar to go back.

The next morning I went to my sister's house. As we were talking I told her that I was really annoyed about losing my glasses. She started to look at me in a strange way and then got really excited. She told me she'd stumbled across a pair of glasses when she'd been in town the previous evening and had just known she had to pick them up. She'd brought them home with her. As soon as she said this, we both knew that they were my glasses. I was so happy that she'd picked them up and that I could now see again.

This brother and sister shared a similar frequency because they were from the same family and so she recognized the extension of his energy before anyone else did. She didn't know what she was doing or why she felt compelled to pick up the glasses, but it was his energy that was attracting her. He hadn't CANCELLED the extension of his energy because he knew he absolutely needed those glasses.

The energy shared between family members is always there and so you will always connect more quickly with someone in your family than you will with anyone else. Here is an experience I had which also shows this family connection:

One evening my son came home really annoyed. He said, 'I've lost my phone, but I've got everything on it – I can't have lost it.'

I suggested I call his number to see if anyone answered. A woman answered and said she had picked up his phone in a Tube station in central London. She had just been trying to find his home number to call him.

I handed my son the phone so he could speak to her. He asked her where she lived – and she happened to live on the same road as us. Through what seemed to be a strange set of coincidences, my son managed to get his phone back within hours of losing it.

My son didn't CANCEL his energetic link to his phone, so it was still an extension of his energy. Also, by sharing energy with him, I was able to stay connected to it as well, and this made the connection stronger. A lot of finders had probably walked past the phone, but this lady shared an energy with him because she lived on our street. People can share energy for all sorts of reasons, as you'll see in this next story:

Shortly after I started university, I lost my purse. Under normal circumstances I would have been really stressed because I was in a large strange city and my purse had lots of important things in, like the keys of my new flat and my university ID card, as well as my money. But it was really weird – I just didn't feel that stressed. I didn't bother reporting it or even checking with Lost Property – as odd as it sounds, I just knew everything would be OK.

That evening when I got home, there on the kitchen table was my purse. A girl from my course had walked 45 minutes out of her way to bring it to me. She wasn't a friend of mine, so I was surprised. All I knew about her was that a lot of people on my course bullied her and she really didn't have any friends. She just seemed to get picked on and left out of things. I'd noticed a kind of sadness in her eyes, so had always made an effort to say 'hello' to her despite what other people thought. I'd been left out of things when I was at school, so I knew how she felt.

Looking back, I don't believe it was a coincidence that this lonely girl had been the one to find my purse and return it to me. I was the only person at university she felt connected to, because I was nice to her.

Even though they weren't friends, these two girls were connected energetically. A lot of people would have walked past the purse, but because the owner didn't CANCEL the extension of her energy, it attracted someone who recognized her frequency.

How to Find Something You've Lost

So, contrary to what you may believe, the way to find something you've lost is not to think about where you might have put it or even to retrace your steps. The key is to stay connected to it and recognize what you do when you are in NEUTRALITY. By doing this, you will be able to find whatever it is you're looking for. It is still an extension of your energy and when you are in a NEUTRAL state the connection remains strong.

All of the stories in this chapter can help you remember when you were in similar situations and found what you had lost. You can then look back at the state of mind you were in. Maybe you thought, 'I can't lose this' or 'I can't be without this.' This is the moment of NEUTRALITY that you move into without even knowing you're doing it.

If you'd like to have a go at playing with being in NEUTRAL-ITY to find something you've lost in a small space, for example your home or office, you can follow these steps:

- Relax and stay calm.

- Don't analyze what you're doing.

- Focus on the fact that you *need* whatever it is you've lost.

- Tell yourself, '*I can't lose this. I really need my... Losing this is not an option.*'

- Walk where your body leads you, without questioning your instinct.

- Look around, move things and pick up things that you wouldn't necessarily pick up.

By doing this, you will be able to find whatever it is you're looking for. Remember, it is still an extension of your energy and when you are in a NEUTRAL state the connection remains strong.

How to Find Your Way

When you are lost somewhere, you can also use the power of your NEUTRAL MIND to find your way. See how I do this:

It was the second time that I was visiting my solicitor in north London. The first time I'd gone in a taxi, so this was my first experience of driving there. After a while I thought I must have gone wrong because I could see some lakes and the area looked dodgy. It all felt a bit strange.

I got in a bit of a panic, so I had to pull over and relax – I know that when I'm in that state I get confused, so there was no point looking at a map. All I knew at that stage was that I had to turn the car around and go back to where I'd come from.

When I was relaxed enough, I waited for the right moment to set off again. I waited until I felt NEUTRAL and knew that I was ready – and I also knew which car to follow to take me in the right direction. I know it sounds a bit odd, but I just knew when to start driving and which car to follow. That car took me right to the road of my solicitor's office.

The strange thing is that the car I followed could, in theory, have been going anywhere – the local supermarket, Oxford, Manchester or central London. But what probably happened was that I picked up on the frequency of a person who was going in the same direction as me. I've done this a couple of times and I'm telling you this to prove a point, so I don't advise you try it – although I'd be interested to know if anyone else does something like this when they're lost!

What can you do when you're lost? Don't worry, you don't have to start following cars. You can do other things to help yourself find a NEUTRAL state so that you can tap into the Super-Subconscious and get the right direction. A friend of mine told me that when he gets lost in his car, he usually opens the window – for some reason this makes him find the right way. What I think is that by opening his window he is unconsciously triggering his intuition.

It Can Be Good to Let Go

Sometimes we need to let go of things that have been an extension of us because we no longer want to stay connected to them. For example, when a relationship breaks up, you may find that when you are truly ready to move on, you get rid of items that hold the extension of that person's energy. You may give away the things they bought you, move out of the home you shared or throw away photos of them. You just know that it's time to move on.

> *I bought a bracelet in Portugal when I was on holiday with one of my boyfriends. I wore it every day, even after my boyfriend and I split up. A few years later I was on holiday again – this time in Greece with a new boyfriend. We'd been to the beach and just as I was getting out of the shower, my boyfriend noticed that my bracelet had gone. I hadn't noticed it myself.*
>
> *My boyfriend was really worried about it and started crawling all over the floor, trying to find it. But I told him not to bother. He couldn't believe I wasn't upset. I just said, 'It was time for it to go.' I had worn it for years, but I felt strangely neutral about losing it.*

Clearly, this woman had let go of any energy to do with that bracelet and so when she lost it she didn't feel as though she'd lost a part of herself. In fact she was liberated by letting go of it and, with it, the last bit of energy of her ex. Her emotional glass was now empty, which allowed it to fill up with a new energy.

You might think that some of the examples in this chapter are just coincidences. But whilst they may seem that way, it's a mistake to dismiss them as nothing more than that. They are illustrations of times when people have successfully connected with the Super-Subconscious – and you have this ability as well. You need to look for times when things like this have happened to you and recognize when you are in NEUTRALITY. You have the power to keep your energy extended to all of the things that are valuable to you and so never have to lose anything again.

CHAPTER 6

Distance Healing

Some people find distance healing a difficult concept to grasp, but what you'll soon understand is that you are already able to communicate in this kind of way. Distance healing is a form of mass energy and it is a two-way process: the role of the person being healed is as important as the role of the healer. I know that some of you will have already experienced distance healing, either with me or someone else, but for others, this will be a new idea. So I'm going to start with an explanation.

What Is Distance Healing?

The easiest way to understand distance healing is to compare it with something that is already familiar to you – radio waves – as healing energy communicates over distance in a similar way.

Transistor radios used to be the most common wireless communication device, picking up signals from aerials at a distance. But today the technology behind the basic radio is the foundation for almost every 'wireless' device: mobile phones, cordless phones, pagers, microwave ovens, televisions, GPS systems, wireless clocks, garage door openers, baby monitors, wireless networks and satellite communication. In these examples, energy doesn't know whether it's travelling a few yards or several hundred miles – and the same goes for healing energy.

All of these technological innovations have been created by human beings, but not only do our minds have the capacity to invent things like these, they also have the ability to communicate in the same way. I first discovered this by accident. I was treating people in my office quite soon after I had discovered my gift. One of my colleagues came into the room and I motioned with my hand for him to lie on the couch. He jumped in shock and said, 'I felt that!' My energy was already channelling into him just by me directing him across the room. I was quite used to unusual things happening at this point in my life, so it didn't seem ridiculous to me.

Then I started experimenting by working on people with my hands just a few inches away from them. Then I tried from across the room, then I moved to the next room and soon I was working on people in countries all over the world.

It didn't take me long to work out that space wasn't an issue and I built up the confidence to work on people whatever the distance. Now I have sent healing all over the globe, including Argentina, Sweden, Japan, Australia, America, Singapore and New Zealand. I have proof that distance healing can be as effective as when I am working directly with someone – but it's not just up to me to make this work. Distance healing is a two-way process and the person RECEIVING the healing is also active in the process and has to be aware of the time when it is happening.

The following case shows how you can have a positive distance healing experience wherever you are as long as you are open to RECEIVING it:

I had been suffering from arthritis in my left knee for some time and, although I'd seen Seka in person before, it was not always easy for me to travel, so I jumped at the chance of having distance healing. I was amazed that I got the same feeling around the top of my head that I had had when she had put her hands on me. I also felt some pressure around my knee, as if the energy knew exactly where to focus.

After the three days of distance healing, my left leg could bend further than it had done in years. It felt stronger and I was able to put my weight on it and walk upstairs normally. Now, ten days later, I can sit normally without having to have my leg straight out in front of me like I used to. I can also swim strongly and am walking for longer.

This is amazing!

Here is a story of someone who was sceptical but who also managed to stay in NEUTRALITY because they didn't have any expectations:

I have suffered with recurrent bouts of cystitis for most of my adult life and after getting increasingly worse over several years, I was finally diagnosed with interstitial cystitis. This is a painful bladder condition for which there is no known cure. A friend told me about Seka and I was initially sceptical. But I had nothing to lose at this point and was prepared to do anything. I tried to keep an open mind and made a five-day block of appointments.

First of all the pain ebbed a bit and then a few days after the healing it got worse and became more of a burning sensation. I panicked and called the clinic. I was told to rest quietly at 9 p.m. that night when Seka would do some distance healing. Never having done anything remotely unconventional like this before, I went along with it, not really knowing what to expect.

I got ready for bed and opened my window wide, even though it was freezing outside. I just felt I needed to do that. I lay on top of my bed and placed my hands over my sore bladder and at just after 9 p.m. my whole body started to heat up and the pain just went. After nearly half an hour I got up and closed the window and felt very warm and comfortable. That night I slept for eight hours without waking – something that had not happened for five years.

Since then I have not had a bout of cystitis, which is incredible. It's a blessing to be free of antibiotics, as I was taking regular doses before, and so I feel so much better.

This was one of the most surreal experiences I've ever had and it will stay with me for a very long time. My profound thanks must go to Seka for being instrumental in this and hopefully for my return to normal health.

This woman had no expectations about what was going to happen and so it was easy for her to be in a NEUTRAL state. By opening her window, she was also almost giving a sign to herself to open herself to NEUTRALITY. Finally, by putting her hands over her bladder, she focused her attention on the part of her body where she wanted the energy to go.

How Does Distance Healing Work?

Contrary to what some people believe, distance healing is not all about the healer. It's a collaboration and connection between the person SENDING the healing and the person RECEIVING it. Distance healing is not something that is 'done to you' – you are 'doing it' too, and so, in this way, it is different from direct healing.

When I'm working directly with someone, I am the one in control of the energy and the person I'm working on just RECEIVES it. The healing will work better if they are in NEUTRALITY, but generally they don't have to do anything. This is a bit like everyday communication. If I want to say something to you and you're in the same room, I can just speak out loud and you will hear my voice, whether or not you want to. You can choose to let the words wash over you (and they will still have some impact) or you can really let them sink in by being in a NEUTRAL state.

Now let's look at how we communicate over distance. Imagine that I am in London and you live in New York. When I want to say something to you, I need to ring you up. But I can't just dial your number, start speaking and expect you to hear me: you have to answer my call. Once you've done that, you can then choose to let my words wash over you or you can really listen to what I'm saying.

In distance healing you also have to actively connect with me as much as I am actively connecting with you. I 'make the call' by SENDING energy and you 'answer' it by being open to RECEIVING it at the time we agree. It's the same process whether you are in the next room to me or on the other side of the world: as long as you 'pick up my call', we can communicate energetically.

Once you connect with me, *you* then control how much you let the energy work by being in the right state of mind. Just as I can't speak to you if you don't answer your phone, I can't heal you if you aren't open to connecting.

As with all aspects of working with energy, you already know more about this kind of two-way communication than you think. There have probably been times in your life when you have been unwell and have connected energetically with someone who was trying to make you feel better. For example, when you were a child, what did your mother or father do? I'm guessing they did things like cuddle you, stroke your hair, tell you lovely stories, and generally give you attention and love. As an adult, people may have bought you fruit or flowers, sent you cards with positive messages and held your hand to comfort you. If you didn't want to accept any of these gestures or gifts, you didn't have to, but you could also choose to open yourself up to RECEIVING the good energy that people were SENDING to you and this is similar to the way in which you RECEIVE distance healing.

Another way this energy works is when you RECEIVE positive energy from musicians when you go to a concert or from actors when you go to the theatre. These performers SEND you energy from a distance.

As you will see later on in this chapter, the most important thing you can do when you are RECEIVING distance healing is to be in a NEUTRAL state, as this opens up your communication channel. You need to clear your mind and not have any expectations – just go with the flow. You are already making choices all the time about whether or not to open up to people and whether or not to communicate with them. It's the same in a healing relationship.

The other critical thing you need to do is to know what you want to get out of the healing. To keep with the metaphor of speaking over the phone, if you don't know what you want to say to me, our communication will get blocked. But if you know what message you want to SEND back to me, we can communicate clearly. You also need the same level of clarity to get the best results from distance healing. Although energy will naturally want to go to the part of you that needs most help, if *you* put your attention on that part of your body too and are open to RECEIVING, you will help the energy come through. If you remember, the woman who had cystitis put her hands on her bladder, which helped her focus her attention. The healer is SENDING the energy, but you are very much in charge of how your body reacts in the process.

The Practical Aspects of Distance Healing

Just as I can't ring you unless I have your telephone number, so you can't be healed from a distance without me having a way to connect with your energy. When I know someone, I know how to connect to their energy, but if I have never met a person before, I ask them to send me a photograph. I need a picture of someone to connect to their frequency or a sample of their handwriting or an object that they're attached to, because all of these things are extensions of their energy.

In order to connect properly, time is also an important factor because the person involved needs to be aware that I'm working on them. By agreeing a time to connect, the RECEIVER and I both open a line between us that allows our energies to connect. As long as the RECEIVER is open to experiencing healing at the designated time, they will RECEIVE the healing energy, regardless of where they are.

Worldwide Group Distance Healing

Over the last few years I have organized three-day worldwide distance healing sessions as an experiment to show people how we can connect with the same energy at the same time. The number of people involved can be in the thousands. Everyone who is involved has a picture of my hands, which is like having my telephone number. They then connect with *me*, as it's not possible for me to have photos of all of them. You can see a picture of my hands at the back of this book and you can use these to connect to the healing energy the next time I am doing this kind of event.

By connecting to my hands, the people receiving healing are the ones who make the first connection – and even if they're not aware of it, they are able to do it. This is the part that you all already know how to do! When someone connects to my hands, it's as though they are calling me, and when I RECEIVE their message, I SEND energy to them. So this kind of distance healing is initiated by the RECEIVER, not by me.

As the numbers of people increase, the energy gets stronger and stronger. When hundreds or thousands of people are all connected to the energy channel, they are also connected to one another, and so we all create a network of energy. You can think of this being like the electrical grid system of a country, whereas when I'm healing someone directly the circuit is like a smaller electricity circuit in a home. So, because of the size and power of the connection in worldwide group distance healing, people can have incredibly strong experiences when they take part in it. Some find that they levitate, while others get very strong images.

As time is always an important factor in distance healing, when I'm working across the world in multiple locations, I use an astrologer to decide the best time for energy to open up in this way. She uses planetary and universal charts to determine the best time of year for everyone to benefit, right to the exact minute. There are very few times in the year when it is safe for me to SEND energy to this extent and for everyone to be able to RECEIVE it; sometimes I even have to wait two months from the time I want to work for it to be ideal and safe for everyone.

The Results of Distance Healing

The main difference between direct and distant healing is that when I work on someone directly, *I* am controlling the energy and the power going into the person because I focus on the specific areas in their body that need work and they just RECEIVE it. But when I work on someone from a distance – either one person or a group – *they* control the energy and how much they take in. This is determined by how NEUTRAL they are at the time.

Whilst energy will always get through to people and work on them to some extent, the degree of success of the healing depends on the RECEIVER controlling the amount of energy they want to RECEIVE – and the way for someone to really benefit is to be in a NEUTRAL state. If they let their mind drift off or they over-analyze, are frightened or fretful, watch the clock or are worrying about anything, they will interrupt their state of NEUTRALITY and won't have the best experience they can. If, on the other hand, they are really relaxed, open-minded and in a NEUTRAL state, it's as if they not only pick up the phone but are also in an area with really good coverage! They just have to lie down and go with the flow...

In the worldwide sessions, the power of the energy is always the same and the distance doesn't matter – you can be in the next room or on the other side of the world. So when people report very different experiences, it's because *they* have been in different states of mind. The following few examples will give you an idea of how much you can affect your own healing experience.

A few days before the first worldwide healing session, my GP told me that I had gallstones. I was really quite upset by this and was also in a lot of pain. During the three sessions, I just lay down and relaxed with my hands on the picture of Seka's hands and let myself drift off to a really relaxed place. I felt some pain and movement in the area around my gallbladder and liver. I could also feel strong waves of heat coming off the picture of Seka's hands.

The following week my GP sent me for another scan, expecting to still see the stones, but there was no sign of them! They had all gone – and so had all the pain! My doctor couldn't believe it, but I could. (Holland.)

I had had varicose veins in my right leg for years. I had always wanted to get rid of them, but had never done anything about it. When I got the chance to take part in Seka's worldwide distance healing session, I was thrilled.

During the sessions, I had some discomfort in my right leg and felt pressure around it. This happened every day. Then during the week afterwards, my leg turned red all over. Then after this, the veins disappeared. Now it's as if they had never been there. (UK.)

You can see from these stories that your physical state doesn't matter. The thing that makes the real difference is your mental state. The two women in these cases were both completely NEUTRAL about what was going to happen. They both relaxed as much as they could, even when they felt some pain or discomfort.

The next case shows how when someone is desperate about their condition they block the energy to that area, yet can still have a good experience in another part of their body:

I lay on my bed for each of the three healing sessions and tried to relax. My hands were very hot for the first 15 minutes and I also had a tingling feeling in the middle of my forehead.

Ten minutes after the healing had finished, I was going to take a painkiller for my back, as I had been doing ever since I injured it in an accident six months before. But I realized that my back no longer hurt. A week later, it is still pain-free.

I'm pleased that my back is better, but the strange thing is that I really wanted to have the healing for my psoriasis. I have been desperately trying to sort this out but it has not changed, even though I kept thinking about it.

Thank you so much, anyway. Next time, hopefully my skin will get better too! (Spain.)

This story shows that energy will get through to someone to some extent regardless of how they feel, but *they* control where it goes. This man was so desperate about his skin condition that he was not able to remain NEUTRAL about it and so blocked the energy from working on his skin. He still got some benefit, however, even though it wasn't in the area where he wanted it most. If he had just relaxed and been NEUTRAL about RECEIVING the energy everywhere, he would have had a better result.

One of the most common sensations people feel during healing is intense heat, especially coming off the images of my hands. This shows that they have made a connection with the energy, but sometimes this is as far as it goes:

About 10 minutes into the session, I felt a surge of heat in my hands and they also turned a dark red/purple colour. The heat lasted a few minutes and then when the session was over I felt very calm and warm. (UK.)

I felt a constant flow of energy and warmth coming from the picture of Seka's hands. It felt like waves flowing up to my head. It was really noticeable and was a lovely experience. (Argentina.)

These types of experience are common and confirm that the person is RECEIVING some energy and has made some connection with it, but if they *only* get a relaxing, warm experience it's because they are not relaxed or NEUTRAL enough. When people only experience warmth, tingling and sometimes pain in their hands, it is usually because they are concentrating really hard on connecting with *my* hands. If you do this, and analyze the process, or worry about whether or not you're doing it correctly, you can block the energy from going any further into your body. Just as a glass has to be empty for you to pour water into it, so you have to make space in your body and mind for the healing energy to work.

If you remember, all of the people whose stories are given here were taking part in the same session and so they all had the same chance of controlling their experience. It was their thoughts and state of mind that made the difference for them.

Healing Can Be More Than Physical

Finally, I want to share with you a slightly different healing experience:

> *I've been a social smoker for nearly 20 years. I've always justified my habit by the fact I take care of my health in all other areas of my life, but in the last year I decided that I should really give up. I tried a few times but always went back to social smoking.*
>
> *It only crossed my mind on the third day of Seka's worldwide healing session that I could try and see if she could heal habits as well as physical problems. So, during the session, I kept thinking about my intention to give up smoking. I was very relaxed and felt the energy come through really strongly. It was like an electric shock and my body even started twitching. It was quite strange, but I felt fine afterwards.*
>
> *The best thing is that I had no cravings at all after the session. One month on, I'm thrilled that I still haven't touched a*

cigarette. I've even been around smokers and have not felt at all tempted to have a cigarette. I have to say that I'm amazed. The cravings I've had for nearly 20 years have finally gone. (Germany.)

This man took the right approach to focusing on what he wanted – he thought about his intention to give up smoking and was open-minded about trying. He had no expectations and so it was easy for him to be in NEUTRALITY.

What you can also see from this case is that you don't have to be physically ill or have an injury to benefit from healing. You can work on any issue where you're experiencing a block or a sense of 'stuckness', such as a relationship, work issue or a habit.

It's amazing that all of this healing can happen just by people connecting with one another. You don't always have to go to a doctor or a hospital or take medication: whilst these things are all sometimes necessary, there are other times when you just have to use the knowledge and ability you already have to heal yourself.

Take Control

Every single person has the chance of taking in energy and experiencing healing when they connect with healing energy, so everybody is equal in that respect. The choice is up to the individual.

In group healing, the mass energy gets very strong and so some experiences are very powerful. Some people are in such a strong state of NEUTRALITY that they get vivid images of me. The last time I did worldwide group healing, one woman emailed me to ask whether I was looking at a map of the world during the session – and I had been. It was as if she'd been watching me on TV! This kind of ability is often called 'remote viewing'. Some people also know exactly when I start and stop the sessions. Once I did five minutes longer than I had originally planned and people from several different countries emailed the office to ask if this was the case, because they'd felt the change at the exact moment I'd stopped connecting.

I work with this energy all the time and so I am very aware of these experiences. It amazes me that people can ignore these kinds of signs. You can't ignore information like this because it is important and these are the signs that prove that you know more than you think.

People who are in NEUTRAL MIND find that they get the best results because they don't question things – they just get drawn to things that feel good. As I have said before, you were born with the ability to be NEUTRAL. Children are naturally open-minded before they start to be affected by the world and so they often get unusually positive healing experiences – even when they don't know what they're doing. You can see this in the next story:

> *I had just finished taking part in your healing session and gone to get myself a glass of water. When I went back into the living room, where I'd been sitting for the session, I saw my daughter holding her hands on top of the picture of your hands. I asked her what she was doing. 'I'm warming up my hands, Mummy,' she said. (USA.)*

This little girl was naturally drawn to the picture of my hands without questioning anything and she felt straightaway what she should feel. She didn't have any idea, preconception, anxiety or expectation about what she was doing; she was simply drawn instinctively to the energy of my hands – even after the 'formal' healing session was over.

Once upon a time, *you* were like this. Your mind was open

to RECEIVING – and you still know how to be in this state. You can look back at the diagrams in Chapter 3 (*page 24*) to remind yourself how your mind works in this way.

CHAPTER 7

We Want to Believe

You saw in the last chapter how your energy extends to your belongings and homes and how these extensions of your energy can be CANCELLED in an instant if you lose your connection to them. Even when your energetic connection is CANCELLED, that energy never goes away, because it can't: energy can never be destroyed, and this also applies to the energy in our bodies when we die. As you may be aware if you have lost someone close to you, the energy of people who have passed away stays with us. The stories in this chapter will help you recognize when you may have already experienced this in your own life.

Our Energy Always Exists

Because energy can never be destroyed, when we pass away and our physical body stops working, our energy becomes part of the universal energy. This energy contains all of the people who have ever walked the Earth as well as all of the knowledge and experience that has ever existed in the universe. Some people think of this dimension of energy as our spirit.

I experienced this for the first time when my mother passed away, because her death was so tragic and sudden. When her energy moved, our home felt completely different because she had spent so much time there and had been the main homemaker. Also, because the way in which she died was aggressive, the shift was instant and dramatic. All of the wooden items in our home split, including the doors and a large wooden vase. These things broke straight down the middle, as if the life had gone out of them – and, in some way, it had. We were left with an empty feeling in the home because my mother's energy had shifted.

I didn't understand what was going on at the time and was scared and confused. As I now know, because my mother's energy was so strong in our home, when her energy moved to the universal level, the extensions of it also moved. I'm no longer frightened when I look back, and I have experienced similar things since and understood them.

An experience I had a while ago was when I was treating a friend of mine who had lung cancer. For two years I visited her every day, even during the weeks she was in hospital, to help relieve her pain and discomfort. One morning when I was at home, a French friend of mine came to see me. I hadn't seen her for nearly 20 years, so I was looking forward to it. The minute she walked into my house, she spotted my piano and rushed over in excitement. She started to play a song which happened to be the favourite piece of music of my ill friend, who also always played that song when she came to my house, so I was shocked when this other friend did exactly the same thing. I knew that this wasn't normal. It was strange how, after not seeing me for nearly two decades, the first thing this woman did was rush to the piano, and so I knew that I was RECEIVING a message from my friend in hospital.

In that very moment I had a rush of heat all over my body. I was burning up and I knew I had to get to the hospital. I didn't have time to explain everything to my friend, but just rushed in a taxi to the hospital. I trusted my instinct; I knew that I had to pay attention to this sign and be with my friend.

As I got to her bedside, she reached out her hand to take mine – and just as our hands touched, she passed away. She had obviously wanted to touch me one more time and it felt such an honour to be there when she died. Her husband was also at her bedside and we shared an overwhelming sense of peace. We even felt guilty about the sense of calm that came over us. To this day, I believe this was because my friend had wanted us to feel at peace, just as she did.

You Can Still Be Connected

When we lose someone close to us, most of us want to believe that person is still with us in some way. This makes us feel better and gives us a sense of comfort, which can help us deal with our grief. My own experience of this comfort has been very powerful.

Up until I lost my mother, I had had a perfect family life. My mother was only 40 when she passed away and I had never dreamed I'd be without her so soon. She was a great influence over our family and a very powerful, charismatic woman. She was gentle and strong at the same time and she exuded wonderful warmth. So when she passed away, for the first time in my life, I questioned what happens to us after we die, and after a while I became more comfortable with the idea of death.

I realized that even though she was gone, Mum was still close to me. I would catch glimpses of her eyes or feel her presence, and warmth would comfort me when I was lonely or upset and I just knew it was her body heat. My mother has helped me through all my difficult times and she's guided me as my healing powers have opened up.

The first confirmation that I had that she was still with me energetically was when I visited South Africa. I had been asked over there by a group of people who were suffering from ME, so I spent the week treating them. One of the patients who came to see me looked like a fairy godmother. She was plump and had a very warm pleasant energy and her presence felt comforting and healing, so I thought I'd have a bit of a play! I thought to myself, 'If you are really a fairy godmother, then I'll ask you three questions that I want my mother to answer to prove she's with me.' I did this in my head as I was treating the woman, but we didn't speak to one another. When I had finished, she said to me, 'I just spoke to your mother. She said I should tell you three things.' She went on to answer the questions I'd asked in my head, exactly as I had imagined. I felt so happy! I was then sure that my mother was with me and this felt amazing.

The next day, the woman returned and gave me a doll of a fairy godmother that she had made by hand. It was as if she had read my mind. I found out later that she ran a Spiritualist church.

I had guessed before that event that my mother was with me, but then I knew for sure. I kept that doll for about 15 years and then one day it disappeared.

It can be very comforting to know that we don't lose someone completely. We can keep a connection with those who have been close to us; they may not be near us in body but they remain with us energetically – and the signs of this can come in some unusual ways.

Last Christmas, my sister invited all of our family to her home. She gave each of the women in the family a beautiful silver bracelet with a dove-shaped charm and the inscription 'Peace 2009'. We all loved them. Tragically, a few months later, she died in a ski accident. Her death was a complete shock to everybody – and whilst I treasured the last gift she had given me, I didn't yet know how meaningful that gift was to become.

In the following weeks, I found myself cooking things I would never have cooked before. But they were recipes that my sister used to make and it made me feel connected to her – as if she was cooking for me. One day, when I was in the kitchen of my country home, I saw two doves together in the garden, and they came back day after day. I had a deep sense that these were my sister and late father and it made me feel so connected to them and comforted by their presence.

Also, at around the same time, I received a call from the producer of a film I had made 15 years before, telling me that she still had the award I'd won for acting in that movie. When she brought it to me, it was in the shape of a dove – and not only that, but inscribed on the award was the title of the film: Sister, My Sister. I could scarcely believe my eyes. I was amazed and knew that it was my sister sending me a message again.

Through connections like this, I know my sister is still with me and I can see the messages she is sending me.

This incredible story shows we can RECEIVE messages in unusual ways. After someone leaves this world, their energy stays with those who were closest to them, even though it's in a different dimension. The physical body can die, but energy does not go away, so our lost loved ones are always with us in an energetic form. We shouldn't ignore these signs, because they're real.

Memories are also energetic connections to other people, so every time we think of someone who has passed away, we connect with them. This can really help us with the grieving process too, as we are experiencing something new and special with these people.

My best friend was obsessed with feathers. Her quilts, cushions and pillows were always feather ones – and I used to laugh at her all the time for being a feather-addict! Even one of the last photos we had taken together was with a feather boa laced around our necks.

She sadly died of cancer three years ago, but since her death I have often found feathers that remind me of her. Sometimes my house seems to be full of them, and whenever I clean I find them scattered about in odd places. I even found one in my work uniform pocket one day – and another time I came across one in my car. Whenever I find these, I always smile and feel warm inside.

I know this isn't a sign that I'm going crazy. I know it's because my friend is still here with me and she wants me to know.

Whilst our lost friends may no longer be around in body, they can still play a part in our life. This next story shows how the messages we RECEIVE from those who have passed away can be things that they want to tell us. They are still observing us and want us to be OK.

My cousin passed away last spring, leaving our whole family in shock. During the two months running up to his passing, when I knew about his illness, I had a colossal fight with a sculptress with whom I share my studio space. She bullied and harassed me to such an extent that I nearly gave up my studio space, but thanks to all the other artists in the studio supporting me, I decided to stay. I know I played a role in the fight, because I never shy away from an argument, but unfortunately the com-munication between us remained icy. During the months that this argument was playing out, my cousin was fighting for his life and I had recurrent dreams about butterflies.

A few days before my cousin passed away I had another dream. This time a whole colony of multi-coloured butterflies flew past me in the formation of a suitcase. It felt like a mes-sage from my cousin, saying that he would soon be travelling. The vision was so real that I could feel the air move softly over my skin as the butterflies brushed past before they disappeared around a big white wall.

The next day I spoke to a friend who lives on a houseboat on the Thames. I told her about my problem with the sculp-tress and my vision with the butterflies. She advised me to overcome my ego and to give my former friend flowers to clear the air. While we were talking about my dream she noticed a golden brown butterfly trapped inside her veranda. We both got the shivers and goose bumps. It was uncanny, because during all the years she has lived on that boat she has never seen a butterfly inside. She opened the window and let him fly away.

Ten days later, after my cousin's funeral, my husband and I spent a night in a hotel on our way to visit friends for a holiday. The next day, as we were having breakfast in the morning room, I noticed a golden brown butterfly beating its wings against the upper window. We got up and opened the window to set it free.

Weeks later, after we'd returned home from our holiday, I got in contact with the sculptress and we decided to meet up in the studio. I took a bunch of pink roses from our garden and I wrote a poem about a stone angel that I had bought from her some time ago. After reading the poem, she cried. We hugged and made up, and out of nowhere a golden brown butterfly flew around us. The sculptress opened the window and as we watched it disappear round the corner, I shivered.

As I'm writing this now, I have shivers running down the left side of my body, as if my soul is being touched. I am convinced that the butterflies were a message from my cousin. Like me, he never shied away from a big fight, but he seems to be saying now that life is too short for quarrels and that we should all try to put aside our differences and forgive each other and ourselves. His message seems to be that we will find peace in our hearts by forgiving.

Funnily enough, after seeing that third butterfly, I haven't seen a single one since.

The way in which you connect with those you've lost is to be in NEUTRALITY. Intend to make contact with the person and, as you do this, you will SEND an energetic message for them to RECEIVE. They are there, so they will RECEIVE it.

My father recently died of cancer and on the day he died my husband and I were having dinner together and talking about him. The day before, we had bought a new lamp for our sideboard. While we were eating, I started thinking about the stories I'd heard of people who'd passed away communicating with those who were left alive. I thought of my father and said to my husband that I wondered what would happen if he wanted to 'talk' to us. I said that maybe he could break our new lamp.

A minute later the lamp clicked and went out. The bulb was broken and even after we switched the bulb, it would not work. It hasn't worked since.

I couldn't believe it and part of me still thinks it was a coincidence. But deep down both my husband and I had the thought that it was my father. He wanted us to know that he was still here.

Although this lady was still tempted to put this down to chance, she knew that it was too meaningful to be just coincidence. She wanted to communicate with her father but had no expectation and so her father SENT her a message back.

How to Cope with a Loss

If someone you have been connected to for many years, or even your whole life, passes away, it will cause you a huge amount of pain, especially if the death was very tragic or sudden, so it's natural to grieve and it's also natural to feel the loss of that person's physical presence. But if you struggle to move on and only focus on your loss, you can destroy yourself and those around you. You have to rebuild your life and focus your attention on the people who are still with you in body. The people you've lost don't want you to suffer. They want you to be happy, to find a way out of your pain and to look to the future.

Unlike other areas of life, where we can look for the positive to help us find NEUTRALITY, when it comes to coping with the loss of a loved one it is usually difficult and inappropriate to look for the positive. Instead you need to think about people who love you and who need you and to start caring for them.

This next story shows how destructive a loss can be if you lose sight of what's left in your own life:

> *A friend of mine lost her teenage daughter to meningitis. Her daughter had started by feeling sick and having a headache, but after going to hospital, she had been sent home with an all-clear. This was a terrible error and tragically she passed away.*
>
> *Understandably, her mother found it incredibly hard to cope. She started to take anti-depressants and lost the will to live. It*

was several years before she realized that she had to move on because not only was she destroying herself but she was also destroying her son, husband and other family members. She felt she had nothing left in her life and so needed to realize that she still had a lot to live for. There were people who were still in her life and she couldn't abandon them.

By putting her attention outside her grief, this woman was able to help herself and her family and move on from the death of her daughter.

In my experience, although I was devastated at losing my mother, after the initial shock I put my attention on other things. Along with my brothers, I devoted myself to looking after my father and I also took my mother's place as the main homemaker.

Some people also find that they come out of the most difficult part of their grieving by devoting their energy to helping people in a way that is related to their loss, for example setting up a charity or foundation to raise money for a meaningful cause.

If you are grieving, you should spend time talking to friends, focus on your job and take care of the people who are left in your life. It also helps to share your stories of loss with other people, as it will make you realize that death is a natural part of the cycle of life and everybody experiences it at some point.

You Already Know How to Connect

If you have ever had to deal with the loss of someone you loved or cared about, I hope you can now see that that person is still with you. Their energy still exists and they may well be SENDING you signs that they are OK, whether it is through doves, feathers or fairy godmothers! You may already be feeling their energetic connection, so I hope you now feel confident enough to look for the messages you are RECEIVING. I know that people find great comfort in knowing this and I hope that if you have lost someone you love that you do too.

PART TWO
ENERGY
IN
PRACTICE

CHAPTER 8

The Lightness of Happy Memories

This section of the book focuses on ways in which you can access your own healing powers. The focus of this chapter is about helping you to realize that you have the power to feel light and happy whenever you want. You can do this at any time through the things you do, the thoughts you have and the people you spend your time with – and you can also achieve this lightness by thinking back to happy times. By controlling what you remember, you can put a smile on your face whenever you want and find a place of safety and comfort whenever you feel stressed.

When you travel to your past and relive the best times of your life, you will find yourself in a NEUTRAL state and your energetic frequency also will shift to that positive place as you bring it to the present moment. The energy of that situation is *always* with you in memory, so when you go back to your happy memories you can bring their frequency to the present and relive them, which will help you nourish and heal yourself. Many of these memories may be from your childhood, which is a time when most people were carefree and spent their time playing, having fun and being cared for, but you will also probably have happy memories from other times in your life, when you were with people you loved, having fun, laughing and being out in nature.

Recently, I was lucky enough to actually relive one of my happiest childhood memories. When I was a little girl in Sarajevo, we lived next door to a family who had two girls and two boys. My brothers and I used to play with them and we all got on really well. One of our favourite games was making mud cakes in empty shoe-polish tins. We used to make them look pretty with flowers that we picked from the garden and we entertained ourselves outside for hours with these kinds of games. My family then moved and I went on to move overseas and so over time we stayed in touch only by phone. Then, after the war in my country, I heard that this family had moved to New Zealand and we eventually lost touch completely.

Last year, I went to New Zealand for two weeks to run some clinics and I asked my father if he still had any contact with this family or if he knew anyone who did. He said he didn't, so I arrived on the South Island and decided to Google them. Nothing came up. Then a few days later, my father called and said he'd opened a drawer at home that he hadn't been in for a while and a letter had fallen out that had come from this family 15 years before, so he knew they were in Auckland.

As you can see, the moment I set my mind on finding these friends, things started to happen. I started to SEND and RECEIVE messages about finding them and it turned out to be the perfect time to do this...

I told the person I was staying with in New Zealand that this family was in Auckland and they said that maybe they had changed their name: it ends in 'ic', like mine, but as it is pronounced 'ich' in English, perhaps they'd changed the spelling. We did a search for them by spelling their name like this – and we found a telephone number. I tried it – and it was them! I couldn't believe it.

We were all so excited. They said that in the few weeks before I'd called, they had been reminiscing and had talked about me – this would be because I had already SENT them the message to find me. They had Googled me as well and had found my website and were thinking of getting in touch. I told them that I was soon to leave Auckland but that I'd be at the airport the next day for two hours. As if by magic, they were also going to be at the airport at exactly the same time because they had to meet a friend who was coming back from a trip. And so we arranged to meet.

I hadn't seen these friends for 35 years, but they looked just like they had done when they were children – well, a bit older! We chatted away about our mud cakes and all the great times we had had. We couldn't wait to go back to those happy days before war hit our country. We also caught up on the years that had passed in between, and it turned out that one of the women had a son with the same name as my son. Their children acted as though they knew me and we shared an incredible energy. We all felt amazing and there was a real buzz in the air around us.

We all went back to the past together and flowed in that energy. The result was a very emotional meeting and we had yet another great memory to look back on.

This was one of the best energy experiences I have ever had and I carried that positive energy with me for months after that. Even writing about it has made me feel fantastic all over again. Coincidences like this can't be ignored, because they are more than just coincidences: the signs throughout this story proved that we were all in touch energetically before we actually saw one another in the flesh.

Even if you haven't found long-lost friends in this way, each one of you has memories like this that you can access any time, memories that make you feel warm and light and happy. When you go back to times like this, not only do you access the memory in your mind but you also access the frequency of the memory. It's always been there and *you already know* how to reach it – you may simply need to become more aware of what you're doing when this happens.

How to Relive Your Memories

Each of us remembers things in different ways and we also code our memories by focusing on our sensory experiences. Because memories are personal, I'm going to take you through the different kinds of memories you may have by triggering your senses. This will help you to remember and relive your own happy memories.

Many of us experience our memories as visual records of the past. Photos are all extensions of your energy and because you usually only take photos when you're happy, they are a quick way for you to connect with the positive moments from your life – the people, the places and the events. Also, when you visit old friends or places from your past, like a previous home or an old school, you are reminded of the good times and the good energy.

I think that one of the most powerful things we can do to make our energy shift to a more positive frequency is remember times we have spent outside. There are so many wonderful natural sights like mountains, cliffs, the expanse of the ocean, fjords and powerful rivers that can make us realize what a tiny part of the world we really are. When we think back to times when we were outdoors, we also help to balance out the amount of time we spend in front of computer screens and on the telephone, doing things that are 'unnatural'.

Music is also a wonderful memory trigger. Most of us have special songs and pieces of music that make us smile or laugh.

For example, if you listen to a song from a long time ago you will be able to remember who you were with, where you were and what was going on around you at that time. Also, because of the powerful energy that music carries, people often use it to distract themselves during difficult times, such as times of war and struggle.

Food is also a fantastic memory aid and memories can be triggered by both taste and smell. There will be certain things you used to eat or that someone used to cook for you and by making these recipes or by eating these foods again, you will relive those cherished moments. One of my strongest food memories from my childhood is my mum's home baking. She was a fabulous cook and I have vivid memories of our family gathered around the kitchen table. She used to make the most wonderful poppy-seed bread and the fluffiest doughnuts in all shapes and sizes. I can smell them now and feel their soothing texture in my mouth. The smell would greet me as I got home from school and I couldn't wait to wash my hands and get to the table. Whenever I need comfort now, I think back to the sweet smell of yeast and the warmth of the kitchen: the memory feels like a soft blanket.

Other smells that could be evocative for you are: the smell of the sea, the perfume or aftershave of someone special, baby lotion, fresh coffee, or the smell of a cake as it's coming out of the oven.

Sometimes it's also important to revisit memories to see them in a different light. When we're children things happen to us that we can't make sense of at the time, but when we look back as adults we realize that things weren't as we thought back then. When this happens, we can see that memory differently and change its energy.

For instance, I remember going to my cousins' house as a little girl to play with my cousins. My uncle had bought presents as a treat for us all and the eight of us ran up to get them. But there weren't enough to go round, and I was the one who missed out. I was so upset to be the only one who didn't have something special to play with and I couldn't understand why I had been left out.

That memory stayed with me for years and I would get upset any time I felt I was forgotten or left out, as it would remind me of the day I hadn't got a present. But looking back as an adult, I could see that my uncle hadn't meant to do that; he probably hadn't counted properly and it was just because I was the last one to run up to him that I didn't get a toy. To the little girl I was then, it was the end of the world, and if I hadn't looked back in later life as a rational observer, I might have left myself vulnerable to any situation where I might feel left out, but I can look back now and rationalize it and laugh.

You Are in Charge of the Way You Feel

You already know more than you may think because you will have been using memories to change the way you feel for most of your life. You just may not have realized it before – or quite why it changes the way you feel. You may also have been thinking back not only to positive memories but to negative ones too – and so hopefully now you can recognize what you're doing and make the right choice. By taking a few minutes to daydream, you have the power to change your frequency and how you feel at any time. You can step into the past and relive the lightness of those happy memories whenever you want and CANCEL the bad ones.

I want to finish this chapter with a particularly heartwarming story of how you can use the frequency of positive memories to change how you feel at any stage of your life:

My husband and I decided that we would take his mother and my father on holiday. At this point, my father was 86 and my mother-in-law was 90 and it was a big thing for them to go on holiday. When people get very old they can often be afraid to leave the safety of their own space and routine: their world shrinks, and the idea of travelling and adopting a new routine, even if only for a few weeks, can be disturbing. But we managed to convince them that it would be a good thing and spent the first couple of days helping them settle in. We showed them that although they were in a strange place, they still had everything they needed, and we made sure we looked after them well. After they had settled, we invited the rest of our families to join us – our brothers and sisters and their children – because we thought it would be lovely for us all to spend time together.

A couple of days later we were all heading out to the swimming pool and my father decided that he wanted to have a go at swimming. Due to an accident many years ago and the fact he is very old, he finds it hard to walk, so this was a big thing for him to do. But once he got in the water, he was able to swim really well because the water was supporting him. He looked so happy being free and feeling strong, and started to remember how he used to feel when he was younger.

With his confidence up and the energy of his past memories to boost him, he then decided that he wanted to dive under the water. We weren't sure what he'd be able to do, but he surprised us all by swimming the whole length of the pool (about 49 feet) underwater! We were shocked and so happy – as he was – and everybody started clapping and laughing.

In all this excitement, none of us had noticed that my mother-in-law had disappeared. A few minutes later she appeared in her swimming costume, which she had not worn for 60 years: she had decided to have a go at swimming too! She started off very slowly and then got stronger and more confident and soon the two of them looked young and happy. Cameras were flashing as we encouraged them – and soon we were drinking champagne to celebrate their achievements. The rest of us then jumped in the pool and we all started acting like we were kids. We splashed and laughed and threw a ball around – and the atmosphere was amazing.

Not just on that day, but for the rest of the holiday as well, we experienced the most beautiful energy. Our parents came out with us every evening until late and had so much energy. Everything felt just right and I felt so alive and happy – as if I could do anything I wanted to.

CHAPTER 9

You and Your Relationships

Some of the most important things in our lives are the relationships we have with friends, family and partners. These relationships are created by energetic connections and so all of the concerns we have about relationships – how to attract them, how to make them better and how to end ones we no longer want – can be addressed by becoming aware of the messages we are SENDING and RECEIVING. When you are able to recognize what is already going on between you and other people, you can protect yourself from energies that are wrong for you and attract people with the right energy.

The Energy of Friendship

The reason why we are drawn to spend time with certain people is not just because we are compatible with them or because we have certain interests or things in common – true lasting friendships are based on two people sharing a similar frequency.

For example, I have a friend I only see once a year but when we see each other we pick up where we left off and it's as if we had only seen each other the previous day. Once it had been about a year since we'd been in touch and I got an urge to give her a call. For days, other things happened, so I didn't have time to call her. Then I went to have lunch in a restaurant that I only visit from time to time. Just as I was about to call this friend, I looked up to see her standing in front of me. I couldn't believe it and she looked shocked too! Not only was she standing there, but she also told me she really wanted to see me to talk about something – and, as if by magic, there I was.

You may think it's just incredible that both my friend and I were trying to find each other at the same time when we hadn't been in touch for so long. But what happened on an energetic level is that we SENT messages to each other about where we were going to be and so we were unconsciously drawn to the same place without knowing why until we got there.

Here is another story about this kind of communication. It was emailed to me after one of my worldwide distance healing sessions:

I have been suffering badly from ME for two years and this evening at 7:20 p.m. I got a really strong urge to lie down on my bed. I didn't know why but I just knew I had to do it. I lay there for half an hour and visualized my body healing and feeling stronger. When I got up, I felt so much better.

When I went back downstairs, I saw that I had three missed calls from a really close friend of mine. I listened to his messages and he had called to tell me about Seka's distance healing session that was taking place at 7:20 p.m. for half an hour. He was telling me that I had to take part. Even though I hadn't answered his calls, his message had got through to me anyway.

I think this is an incredible example of how we SEND and RECEIVE messages. This man's friend didn't need to ring him up because, just by thinking about it, he had already SENT the message. Without knowing what he was doing, his friend had RECEIVED it and acted on it. So, if we all tapped in the Super-Subconscious, maybe we'd never need to use a phone again!

This next story shows how we can also communicate through objects that are an extension of our energy – and how this energy interacts with the frequency we share with our friends and family:

Last week I was dusting an ornament that was a gift from a friend. I was thinking about her and all the good times we've had, and as I placed it back on the shelf, my phone rang. It was my friend! We hadn't been in touch for weeks. We laughed at the story and she now calls that ornament my 'magic lamp'. She says that anytime I want to talk to her, I can dust it and she'll call.

By thinking about her friend, this woman SENT a message to her to get in touch. Her friend then picked up the message and called.

Sometimes these energetic connections can also happen between groups of friends who are close to one another. One evening I was thinking about a friend of mine who had lost her sister very suddenly. I was concerned about how she was coping. At the exact moment that I was thinking about her, I received a text from her saying she wanted to come for a treatment.

Then, after I had treated her, she asked me if I could also see her mother. I said, 'Of course,' and we walked into the waiting room. At that moment my secretary said to my friend, 'You'll never guess what? Your mum just called to make an appointment for you, but I told her you were in with Seka.'

Whilst this could just seem like a series of coincidences, there was more than chance at work. In this triangle of energy, we SENT and RECEIVED messages to and from each other because we were all supporting and caring for one another. The energetic frequency had a ripple effect and connected the three of us.

This kind of communication often happens between family members. I have a strong a bond like this with my father and we often communicate through our shared energy. He even knows when I'm in trouble. Once, for example, I was on my way to a wedding in Mallorca, but because of an immigration mix-up, I ended up in prison. I remember feeling really angry, as well as scared and confused. I was put in a small cell for hours and I knew there was nothing I could do about it. I decided to read the newspaper to take my mind off what was happening. I also refused to drink the water or eat the food they offered in protest at being so badly treated. I shouldn't have been there at all and I didn't want to take anything from them. I was in shock. I was frightened and had no idea what was going to happen to me.

After several hours of waiting I was released and the misunderstanding was rectified. Later, when I relayed the horrible event back to my family, I found out that my father had felt my fear and frustration and had been trying to contact me the whole time I had been in prison. He had been really worried about me but hadn't known why. He had just felt that something was wrong with me.

It was extraordinary that my father could feel my emotion from so far away. But I was SENDING out my fear and he picked it up because he was the person closest to my frequency.

Recently, I was part of another energy triangle that spanned the globe. Here's my friend's account of it:

I was catching up with a friend in London for the first time since we had met in Mexico the month before. We were both excited and chatting away when suddenly she mentioned that years ago she had met a healer, but she couldn't remember her name. She said, 'It begins with an "S" and her surname is something like "Nikola", but I can't remember it.' I immediately said, 'Do you mean Seka Nikolic?' and she said, 'Yes!' When I told her that Seka was my best friend, she was so over the moon she burst into tears, saying, 'I can't believe it. She helped my son so much many years ago. She's the best healer I've ever met. I really wanted to find her again.' I was so overcome as well that I also started crying. It was a very special moment.

The next day, I called Seka to tell her and to book an appointment for this friend. I found out afterwards that just as I was leaving her a message on her mobile, Seka was asking her secretary to give another patient my phone number because she wanted to learn Tai Chi from me. Also, at exactly the same moment that this was happening, Seka's secretary received an email from the friend I'd met in Mexico, who had tracked Seka down herself! Everything came together in the same second.

We shouldn't ignore stories like this. It's important to pay attention to them to prove to ourselves that we already use the power of our energy all the time.

I love these kinds of stories and I remember all the ones that have happened to me. But even though I'm used to this kind of communication happening, I was surprised at this set of events. This woman had been trying to remember my name and track me down for nearly two decades and finally found me through my best friend, who is an extension of my energy. She even followed this energy to Mexico, where she met my friend – and after all this travelling all over the world, all our energies came together in one minute in my clinic. This story shows how when you set your intention and your frequency to make a connection, you can make it happen even against the odds.

It's a natural human desire to want to have things and people in our life that are similar to us. We attract each other by having similar frequencies and, as you can see, this can happen across any distance.

How to Bring Out the Best in People

We don't always have a positive connection with people, of course, and sometimes we can find ourselves in situations where there is a negative energy. If you are ever in this kind of situation you don't have to give in to that energy and connect to it. You can protect yourself by refusing to RECEIVE it.

One night many years ago in my country I was getting a late train back into the city. I was waiting on the platform with two dodgy-looking guys. Apart from the stationmaster, who popped out of his office every now and again, nobody else was around. When the train pulled in to the station, I got on – and so did the two men. I sat in one carriage and they followed me in and closed the door (it was one of those trains that has separate carriages, unlike the open format you usually see today). One man sat opposite me and one sat next to me. The man opposite me had a big scar across his face from the top of his forehead to his opposite cheek and jaw. I recognized him from somewhere, but I didn't recognize the guy next to me.

At this point, I could easily have panicked and got really afraid, because my instinct told me that they intended to do something to me. But I did the opposite. My survival response told me to relax. I looked across at them, smiled and offered them some chocolate. They looked completely shocked and accepted it – and so we all sat there sharing my chocolate bar.

I was racking my brains to remember how I knew the guy opposite me. Then it came to me: it had been reported in the newspapers that he was a criminal. Still I didn't panic. I just acted as if they were friendly and started chatting to them as I would with anybody. I could see they looked confused at first, but then started to relax and by the end of the journey we were chatting and having a laugh.

It was 3 a.m. when we got to the city and the two guys refused to let me go home alone. They said it wasn't safe for me to be out on my own at that time of night and insisted on chaperoning me home. The guy with the scar told me that he was selling jeans and that I should bring my friends to buy them from him – and so a few weeks later I did. In a strange way, I was grateful to him for not doing anything bad to me. A few months later, he started driving a taxi for a living and abandoned his life of crime. I used his services several times and he never used to charge me. It was as if something in him shifted on that night and he turned over a new leaf.

I don't know exactly what went through the minds of those men that night, but I know that by refusing to connect to the frequency of fear, I didn't do what they expected me to. By not matching their frequency and not reacting as they had expected, I CANCELLED their bad intentions and reset their energy and behaviour. They were not programmed to deal with the energy that I brought and so I reversed the situation.

If I'd let myself be afraid that night, I might well not be alive today. It might not make sense, even now, but I made the right choice. I believe that everybody has some good in them and because I didn't let myself show these men that I was afraid, I gave them the chance to get into the positive frequency they had inside them.

The Energy of Intimate Relationships

Most people want to find 'the One' – a special person with whom they can share their life – and when we talk about good relationships and romantic connections, we often use phrases like 'love is in the air', 'the atmosphere was electric', 'he sent shivers down my spine' or 'we were on the same wavelength'. It is no coincidence that these sayings all talk about the *shared energy* between people.

Often the situations where we feel this connection seem to arise as if by magic, which can make us uncomfortable if we think we're not in control of them – but we are. We use energy to attract people all the time, and we can do it consciously. Even if we're not aware that we are doing it, we are the ones who make attraction happen.

I share a flat with three friends, one of whom is my boyfriend. We all get on well and share most of the jobs around the house, including taking turns to cook, depending on who gets home first.

One day, I went to the supermarket to buy things for dinner and, along with all the other bits of shopping, I picked up my favourite bar of chocolate. It was the last one on the shelf, so I was really pleased. But when I went to pick some apples, I put down the chocolate bar by accident and forgot about it.

As it happened, my boyfriend went into the same supermarket about an hour after me, not knowing that I had just been in there – and I hadn't known that he was going either. As he was passing through the fruit and vegetable section, he spotted my favourite bar of chocolate nestled amongst the apples. He picked it up, knowing I'd be really pleased with him. As you can imagine, when he got home, we shared our experiences and realized what had happened.

This example is only about a bar of chocolate, but it shows how we are continually SENDING and RECEIVING messages through our energy, even through something as mundane as food shopping. This kind of energetic communication can be about anything, be it the thoughts and feelings you have – or a bar of chocolate!

This doesn't just happen between partners. When several women live together, after a time their menstrual cycles coincide and the only explanation for this is the energetic frequency passing between them. Also, if you live with or spend a lot of time with other people, you may find that you start to take on their nature and characteristics. This doesn't just happen at a level of habit (for example how you talk and what you actually do), but also at an unconscious level that you experience as a change in the way you feel or act, such as being aggressive, depressed, stressed, positive or calm. So be careful who you hang out with!

The Choice Is Yours

When someone has been in an unhealthy relationship, for example with a partner who depletes or drains their energy, even if they don't want that kind of partner again, they may still be attracted to people who have a similar energy. You often hear people say 'I always attract the wrong men' or 'I always end up with needy women' – and they're absolutely right. They are unconsciously carrying their fears with them and attracting the same kind of men or women by SENDING out a particular frequency. They'll keep on living that pattern unless they become aware of it. For example, if someone is scared of being abandoned, by focusing on the very thing they don't want they will SEND out that energy and attract it to them – and so will end up again and again with people who are unfaithful.

This kind of pattern often stems from the experiences we have had earlier in life, either as children or in other relationships. For example, if your father was very controlling, whilst you may not *want* to be with that kind of partner, you may attract that frequency and end up with someone like him. Whilst it may not be obvious why you are doing something like this, there is a logical energetic explanation: you are attracting what you *don't* want.

You do, however, have the power to attract a partner who is right for you. To be able to bring who you want into your life, you need to recognize what you are doing and trust your instincts. You also need to recognize the signals that you're SENDING out to avoid getting stuck in a pattern of relationships that don't work for you. This means acting on your instincts: don't ignore the signs early on in a relationship, as you may well look back in the months or years to come and wish you had paid attention to them.

I met a guy at a singles evening and we got on really well. I didn't find him irresistible, but he was attractive enough and I hoped he'd grow on me. He seemed to tick a lot of the right boxes. On our second date, he cooked me a lovely meal at his flat and I commented on how nice his place was. I was a bit surprised at the décor and style of it, because it seemed a bit old-fashioned and 'girly' and he was not that kind of guy. So I asked him how long he'd lived there, assuming he'd only recently moved in, and he said he'd bought the flat the year before.

A couple of weeks later he told me that his rental contract was up for review and started hinting that he could move into my place. I remember feeling really upset that he'd lied to me about owning his flat, but I didn't make a big deal of it because I didn't want to rock the boat. He also said that when I'd asked him about his flat he'd felt pressured to say that he owned it. I wouldn't have cared if he hadn't owned it, though. I cared more about him telling me the truth. Nevertheless, I decided to give him the benefit of the doubt.

In the end we stayed together for nearly four years – and during that time he lied to me repeatedly about all sorts of things, including relationships with other women. Looking back, I can see that my instinct told me from the moment of that first lie that something wasn't right, but I chose to ignore it. If I'd walked away then, I could have moved on quickly; as it was, our break-up was a lot messier in the end. I lost four years of my life by not listening to my gut in the first place.

This woman found out too late that her instincts were right all along. She should have acted on that initial feeling of being hurt by this man's lies, but she decided to ignore it.

Many people choose what they want to see in someone, either because they don't recognize how powerful the energetic messages are that they are RECEIVING or because they are afraid of being alone and so ignore their instincts. You can create whatever you want to see and overlook the reality around you, but to find the best person for you, you need to be honest with yourself and be in a NEUTRAL state to allow those messages to come to you. You need to detach yourself from what someone is saying when you first meet and just listen to the facts. If they don't add up or if you have a hunch about someone, you're probably right. You have to recognize what your energy is telling you and pay attention to it.

You Have to Know What You Want

One of the reasons why we often make mistakes and ignore our instincts is because we don't know what we really need in a partner. It's often much easier to go along with other people's concept of the ideal man or woman and get carried away with the things that other people tell us we *should* want. But you have to be honest about what *you* want in a partner, not what you think you should have or what anybody else wants you to have. Too many times people are with the wrong person but can't admit it to themselves, and maybe that's because they're not clear about what they want.

We all need someone who makes us smile, someone with whom we can communicate, have fun, share things and spend our time. But aside from the qualities and characteristics that most people want in a partner, it's important that you *know* what *you* want. You need to think about how you want them to act, what you want them to look like and all the other qualities you find attractive. You can write all of this down if it helps you think it all through. You should also write down where you want to be with that person and imagine yourself in all those places with them. You need to see the life you want to have and who you want to have it with in as much detail as you can.

This exercise might seem simple, but I have known some people, especially those who attract the wrong kind of partners over and over again, who find it impossible to imagine their perfect partner. And until they can do that, they won't bring them into their life.

A few months ago I had a patient who was complaining to me about being single. I asked him what kind of woman he wanted, but he couldn't answer. I asked him, 'Do you want a woman to look after you? Do you want her to be caring? What do you want?' He still couldn't answer me. He just cried and cried and kept on saying, 'I don't know what I want.'

The next day he came back for treatment and said to me, 'Now I know what I want. I don't need a woman to look after me.

I just want someone who's kind.' Again, he started crying, but this time they were tears of joy because he had finally listened to his instinct.

Like this man, you need to take the time to think through what you're really looking for. It may not come overnight, because you may not have any idea about the kind of partner who's right for you. It's worth being patient, so you can choose the right person rather than rush into the wrong matches over and over again.

Having had a bad long-term relationship, a friend of mine spent a lot of time really thinking about what she wanted in a soul mate – and it paid off:

I had recently split up with my long-term boyfriend. If I'm honest with myself, whilst our relationship had been 'good enough' to last as friends, the romance and spark had been gone for a long time. I knew that I really wanted someone truly special to share my life with.

It was New Year's Eve and I decided that I was going to create the intention of meeting my perfect man. I'd thought about it before but never really given it my full attention.

I bought myself some lovely red notepaper and wrote down a description of the kind of person I wanted to meet – kind, generous, affectionate, fun-loving, intelligent, hard-working, honest, mature, responsible, friendly and handsome! I also said that I wanted to meet him by 30 June that year. I don't know why but that date just felt right. I then put the note in an envelope, tucked it in a drawer and forgot about it.

In the coming months, I did a bit of online dating on and off and in May I joined a new dating website. After a few weeks and a few mediocre dates, I started to get bored, and as June drew to a close, I decided I was going to end my membership. But before I did that, I sent a message to a guy who I thought looked nice and who had shown an interest in my profile. I thought I had nothing to lose. He replied within minutes of receiving my message, saying he had been about to email me. It was the evening of 30 June. Two years on, we are living together and very happy.

This woman spent time working out what she wanted and, although she had to make some mistakes first, this helped her realize what she didn't want too. This shows that the frequency of your energy is more important than your conscious thoughts: you have to really want something at a deep energetic level to get it – and when you do, you can even get it on the exact date that you want.

Some people only know what they want when things have got very bad for them: by hitting 'rock bottom' they realize how much they need to change – as this next story shows:

I was 33 when I hit the lowest point in my life. I was in a love-less relationship, was miserable living in London and my job was draining me. It was only at this point, when there seemed to be nothing good in my life, that I decided I'd had enough – I couldn't take any more. I decided that I needed a total overhaul of my life – where I lived, my job and my relationship. Deep inside I knew exactly what I wanted – and I also knew what I didn't want.

Within two weeks (yes, two weeks) I had met a new partner and three months after that, we were married. My husband is from Spain and so now I also have a new home, which suits me so much better. Three months after our wedding, I got pregnant – and so now I also have the new job of being a mum! Everything I wanted came to me.

What you can see from this story is that change can happen immediately when you know what you want. You can tap into the Super-Subconscious in a split-second as long as you are in NEUTRALITY. For this friend, the turning point was the moment she made a decision – and it was at this point that she moved into a different frequency. She told me that she felt lighter as soon as she made up her mind. Even before she had made the actual changes, she had made the greatest change of all: she had changed her energy. Her commitment and the certainty she had that she was doing the right thing meant that she shifted to a NEUTRAL state without even being aware of it. By doing this, she opened the door to a new future.

You Know More Than You Think

To find the right friendships and relationships, you need to recognize the ability you already have to know what's wrong and right for you. The signs are always there: hunches that something is wrong, that feeling of 'love at first sight' and inklings in your tummy that you have to do something. You must pay attention to these energetic messages and not ignore them. When you start to recognize and act on the messages that you are RECEIVING and SENDING, you could bring similar magic into your life.

Almost 20 years ago, when I was very ill with ME, I joined my local ME Association. One day, their newsletter mentioned that a group of people had started to write to others so they could feel supported. It didn't strike me as anything I would be interested in and so I went to bed. But the next morning I woke up thinking about the support group and I felt really excited. My instinct told me that I had to become part of it. I don't know why, but I just did it.

I started writing regularly to a man who lived in England (I live in Holland) and three years later he invited me over. Because we were both so ill, it was hard for us to travel, but I really wanted to go and I knew that soon there would be a way for it to be possible. Sure enough, there was. Just after he invited me, a new airline started flying from my local airport to his. It was amazing, because it made the journey manageable. This was too much of a coincidence. Then, to celebrate the launch of this new route, there was a competition in my local newspaper to win two free tickets to the UK – and something told me that I was going to win. Guess what...? I won.

I went to England to meet my new friend and even managed to get the second ticket transferred into his name so that he could visit me in Holland. When I went to see him, he proposed – and it was like a dream come true.

If I hadn't listened to my instinct all those years ago, I would never have met my husband.

At every step of the way, this woman paid attention to the messages she was RECEIVING and acted on them. She was in a NEUTRAL state, so she didn't question or doubt or worry, she just trusted herself and what was going on – and the result was magical.

You can do this too. As you now know, you are RECEIVING messages all the time; you just need to pay attention to them.

CHAPTER 10

Health and Healing

In my years of practising Bio-Energy, I've seen so many different health conditions, caused not only by accidents, viruses or the environment, but also very often by stress. In fact, something that is increasingly apparent to me is that most illness comes about because of stress and emotional upset, which depress our immunity.

In the twenty-first century, life happens at such a pace that it's hard to keep up. Whilst we think our developed world gives us a better life than before, our quality of life has actually become worse over the years. We constantly feel under time pressure and lack nourishing face-to-face contact with people, as we communicate so much via phone and email. Not only are we distanced from other people but we are also distanced from ourselves: we are so distracted by the external world that we move further away from our own body and mind and start to lose a sense of our own frequency. To be in the best state of health, you have to address what's going on at all levels, inside and outside your body. You have to look not only at your physical symptoms but also at your thoughts, feelings and all other aspects of your health.

You Already Know How to Be Healthy

You already know how to be healthy and you know what it feels like when you are strong and well. When you take the time to listen to and respect your body, you can look after your health.

The most important thing you can do is to make the right choices in your life and give yourself good quality time. Then you will be able to listen to your gut instinct. When you are on the right path, your body will SEND you the signs. Whether it's to do with your job, relationship, home or other choices, by doing what's right for you, you can keep yourself in a NEUTRAL state and your energy at a healthy frequency.

As I have found through healing people, the more you ignore your instincts, the further you get from your natural frequency, or, to put it another way, the more you feel a 'dis-ease' with life, the more you open yourself up to the possibility of poor health. But we all have an intuitive sense of what we should be doing with our life and what's best for us. When we listen to this instinct and follow it, we experience good health – and we do this best when we are in a NEUTRAL state.

Many years ago I had gallstones and my gallbladder became inflamed, so I was in a lot of pain. I was in hospital, wired up to drips, waiting for an operation. I couldn't risk eating or drinking anything other than very weak chamomile tea in case the stones ruptured. I was drifting in and out of consciousness because of the pain and the lack of food. But on the third day, my deep-rooted will to live took over.

The lady in the bed next to me was pregnant and her mother had made some pastries for her. They were a bit like Cornish pasties, only smaller, and there was a whole bagful by her bed. I kept looking at them and the smell was wafting over to me. I'd been told that eating anything could put me in serious danger, so I lay there for while. About five minutes later, though, the urge was just too strong. My body was telling me I had to eat – but it was not a normal hunger like I was used to: it felt like a deep drive to survive, like an animal instinct. It felt as if I would die if I didn't have food.

I heaved myself up off the bed and, with my drip in one hand, grabbed the bag of pastries with the other. All my manners went out of the window. I could barely walk, but somehow I made it to the toilet. I locked the door, sat down and worked my way through what must have been nearly three pounds of pastries. I ate them methodically and mechanically. They were warm, solid and nourishing. It was as if I had never been ill – and as if I'd never seen food before!

Immediately after finishing them, I felt different. I could feel energy filling me up and I was suddenly alert and alive. I left the toilet and walked back to my bed feeling totally present and completely well. There was no pain at all in my body; it was as if I'd never had a problem. Nobody would have guessed that five minutes earlier I'd been practically unconscious. I discharged myself, much to the doctors' surprise.

A few days later I found out that many people who had had operations on that day had died, some of them on the operating table. There must have been a deadly virus in the hospital or something else to cause that. Thanks to my gut and the fact that I followed it, I was still alive.

If I'd stopped to think about what my body was telling me, I would never have done this. I probably would have said that it was silly to eat something so rich when I was so ill, but I didn't analyze it. I was in a state of NEUTRALITY and just followed my instinct. Women often do this when they're pregnant and get cravings to eat certain things. Your body is incredibly clever and when you pay attention to the messages you get, you can heal yourself.

Neutrality Is the Answer

When you get ill, it's common to feel shocked because it can feel as though it has crept up on you from nowhere. The reality is that most health problems take time to develop – they don't happen overnight. However, if you haven't been paying attention to your body, you probably won't have noticed. The initial signs of feeling run down, tired or in pain, for example, can get lost in the rush and bustle of daily life and so it's often only when you get a big sign that you are forced to take notice.

After the truth of a condition sinks in and you have got over the initial shock and upset that most people experience, you must realize that you have two choices:

1. You can decide to be ill and stay frightened of the illness.

2. You can decide to fight it and get better.

    If you decide to fight it, you need to do the following:

- Focus on looking after yourself.

- Pay attention to your body, even if it is a new experience for you.

- Don't let fear make your decisions for you, as fear is usually wrong.

- Find a place of peace and NEUTRALITY in which you can attract the right energy, treatment and people to help you get better: this is the best decision you can make.

- Have a deep belief that you'll be OK. You have to see yourself coming out of the condition – and fighting it.

- Listen to your instinct, as it will tell you what you need to do.

- Distance yourself from your condition by observing yourself and not attaching yourself to it. One of the simplest ways to do this is to imagine you are telling a friend what to do. How would you tell them to look after themselves?

Your state of mind is critical to your health. These next two cases demonstrate how two people with the same condition can apply thought processes differently to their health – and how this affects the healing process:

A woman in her late twenties came to see me with extremely serious eczema. Her skin was cracked and bleeding so badly that she had to wear gloves all the time and her face was so badly affected that it was hard for her to move it to talk properly. When I was treating her I couldn't even touch her. I didn't know whether or not to promise her what I could do, as she had tried every single treatment she could, both medical and alternative, and by the time she'd come to see me, she felt she had nothing to lose.

But, despite her condition, the results I got were amazing. I wish I'd taken photographs, because on each of the five days she came to see me, her skin got visibly better. One week after she had started her treatment with me, it was totally healed. It looked like a baby's. It was quite incredible and she was so grateful.

Two weeks later, a man came to me. He was a similar age to the woman and had a similarly chronic case of eczema. Hav-

ing just treated the woman with such success, I told him that I could really help him and I was confident that by the end of the week he'd look and feel much better. But he couldn't accept this at all. He said to me, 'Nobody can help me. I've spent so much money for so long and tried everything. I don't believe anything can work.'

Each day, however, his skin did get better. It wasn't as quick or as dramatic an improvement the woman's had been, but there was definite progress. All this time the man kept on looking in the mirror and obsessing about his skin. He was looking for every little change that had happened Even though his eczema was better, he still said that he didn't think it would go away completely. By the end of the five days, he was better, but, just as he had said, his skin was not clear, like the woman's had been. I told him to come back two months later

When he came back, his skin was clear! I asked him to tell me honestly when he felt he had really started to heal. He said that two days after he had finished his course of treatment with me, he had stopped obsessing. He had given up any expectation of getting better and this had triggered him to let go of his negativity – and that's when he had started to get better. He had thought I hadn't helped him and so, as I was his last resort, he hadn't bothered staring at himself anymore. He had thought nothing would work, so he might as well stop trying to sort it out. He had stopped looking in the mirror at every opportunity and his mind had started to focus on other things. At that point, when he had stopped thinking negatively about his skin, the healing had happened very quickly.

These two cases show how important your thought processes are when you are unwell – and also how easily they can stop you from getting better. The woman had a very strong survival instinct and wanted to fight her eczema: it was this mindset that helped her get better in five days. But the young man was frightened of getting better and, by looking in the mirror, searching for signs of his eczema, was subconsciously wanting to see signs of it. Also, by telling me that nobody could help him, he was blocking the energy from helping him. At the moment when this man let go of his negativity, he released all of his blockages to the energy and the healing happened in two days.

One thing to learn from this story is that even if you have had negative thought processes before, you can always change them – and change your life for the better.

The Power to Create a Family

Although I treat people for all sorts of conditions, where I see the most fear and desperation is in couples who want to start a family but are having trouble conceiving.

Although it is harder in women who are at an age when their fertility drops, it's usually easy for me to help patients who have physical fertility problems, such as difficulties with ovulation, blocked Fallopian tubes or poor sperm motility. That's the simple part. But the physical healing is only the beginning: I also have to help people work on the thought patterns that are stopping them from being NEUTRAL about having a child.

It's very common to see women who block their own energy and so disrupt their body chemistry. Ironically, they are usually desperate to have a child and it is this desperation that is stopping them. In men, I often see that the pressure they're under to have a baby affects the quality of their sperm. In both cases the most important thing people need to do to have a child is relax, enjoy each other and adopt a NEUTRAL attitude to having a child. The next two cases show how this kind of mindset is absolutely critical:

A couple came to see me about their fertility problems. They were both in their early thirties and very knowledgeable about their health. After many years of trying, they had got increasingly worried and obsessed about the woman not being pregnant, because they had expected it to happen by then. They had put all their energy into having a baby for so long; they had charted and measured everything they could and rigidly scheduled their sex life. What they couldn't see was that they were blocking their energy by behaving like this. They were each SENDING desperate messages to their body that they were afraid of not having a child. Their bodies were picking up on the fear and so their subconscious minds took it to mean that they didn't want a baby. The more they wanted one, the less chance they had: they were caught up in a vicious circle. Whilst they could understand this intellectually, they did not know how to get out of this negative pattern.

I said to them, 'Please believe you will have a child – because you will. Just relax and don't even think about children for six months.' Their bodies and minds were overstressed and they really needed a rest. I wanted them to take a break from the negative thoughts that had been blocking their energy. I suggested they have fun and make love because they loved one another, not just to make a baby. I then told them to try again in six months.

They started going back to life as it has been before. They went out, had fun, made love and were playful with each other. Then, six months later, I received a message from them that they were having a baby. They had released the pressure they'd been putting themselves under when they had started to just enjoy their relationship and intimacy.

A woman in her early thirties came to see me with fertility problems. She and her partner had tried IVF many times but had been told that they should give up because their problems were not solvable. The woman came to me very upset and, because of what she'd been told, with only a tiny glimmer of hope left. She cried during her first appointment and asked me if I could help her. She felt she had nothing to lose. I told her that all I could do was try my best.

After the treatment I told her and her husband to look after themselves and not to expect anything for four months. They'd been under so much stress through having IVF that I wanted them to stop thinking about pregnancy and just have some fun. I suggested they just enjoy each other, as they had done when they'd first met. In this case, she was pregnant within a month!

These two stories show how the most important thing you can do when you want to have a baby is be in NEUTRALITY. Although there was nothing physiologically wrong with the first couple, their energy was all over the place and making it hard for their bodies to work naturally. Ironically, the woman in the second case, who had physical problems, was closer to being in NEUTRAL MIND because she felt she had nothing to lose. All she could do was have hope – which is better than desperation. Having a baby is a natural process and when you treat it as such, it usually happens.

The Pattern of Illness

When your body is healthy, your mind is healthy, but in the case of people who have been unwell for a long time (which includes many of those I work with), their minds are programmed differently. Some of these people (but by no means all) seem to be attracted to an 'illness frequency' because they've been ill for such a long time. Even when their body is better and they are physically healed, their mind may still be used to thinking in a negative way and so they continue to attract negative energy. Most people find it hard to break this kind of cycle – and some of them aren't even aware of it in the first place.

If you have a long-term illness, it can feel that it's become part of your life. It's like a bulky piece of luggage that you carry with you every day, and when it's taken away from you, it can feel uncomfortable, as if something is missing. Some people are very honest with me about this. They say, 'I've had this my whole life. I don't know what to do now.' They are so used to the frequency of their condition that they can't imagine life being different. They say things like 'What if I'm ill again in three months?' or 'What will happen to me now?' When people ask me things like this, I ask them back, 'What will you do if you feel good for the rest of your life?' Usually, they can't answer. They are programmed to be in the frequency of their condition. However, they really can change this by changing how they think.

The hardest cases to work with are people who can't see how they are attracting the frequency of an illness. For some reason, they don't want to believe that they're better, and so, by worrying about what will happen if they relapse, they attract the very thing they don't want.

One condition I often treat is chronic headaches and after a week of being free of these pains, sufferers sometimes say to me that they feel strange without them. They can even miss their headaches! I know that to some people this will sound ridiculous, but I have heard this so many times that I know it's a very real phenomenon.

One of my patients came to see me because she had been having migraines every single day of her life since her teens. After the second session, her headaches stopped. She called up the clinic and was crying hysterically. 'What have you done?' she said. 'I have always had these headaches! I don't know what to do without them.' These were not tears of joy – she really didn't know what to do with herself.

This woman's daily life had been so taken over by her extreme headaches that they stopped her from having to deal with anything else in her life. In fact they provided a huge and convenient distraction from her problems. It turned out that she had been abused as a child and she had always been too afraid to face it, so she had created the pattern of headaches to cover up the pain of her abuse. This was a form of 'self-harm', because she had just replaced one kind of pain with another. Her life had been totally focused on her illness, so when she was free of the physical pain, she didn't know what to do with the emotional pain. But even if something has happened to you as a child, you can get help from qualified mental health professionals to cope with these issues – they should not stop you from being healthy.

When you start to observe your thought processes, you may notice you have two different 'minds'. You may have one that is unquestioning, that is free of expectation and that wants to get better, and you may have one that is afraid, that wants to analyze and that is used to your condition. The more you recognize these, the more you can make the right choices about what you think and can reprogram the relevant mind. You don't have to be affected by what other people think or by what you're told: you can create your own mental state yourself.

Because it can be easy for you to get drawn to the frequencies that you're used to (even when they're doing you harm), I believe that you need to be careful in places where people with the same illness or condition gather together. For example, in some cases rehab groups can end up maintaining the energetic state that sufferers want to move away from, which makes it harder for them to recover. It doesn't mean people *can't* recover in these situations, but they would find it easier if they were surrounded by people who didn't have the same problem. Also, some people with illnesses choose to join support groups, but these groups encourage people to share their negative energy and get comfortable with their condition by making them realize they're not alone. The frequency becomes familiar to them and they find it harder to change. So, if you are ill, you should try to spend as much time as possible with people who have healthier frequencies.

For this reason I also believe that hospitals should have mixed wards, which does happen in some cases. Whilst it might not make sense from an organizational point of view, it really helps patients if they are not with people who share the same problems. By having other frequencies around them, they are less likely to create a mass frequency of illness, which CANCELS the connection to healthy, hopeful energies. You need to be aware of, and may even choose to avoid, situations that maintain a negative frequency. You have to CANCEL the frequency of illness and be ready to attract a healthy one – and the way in which you do this is by attracting new patterns, and new healthy energy, into your life.

The Pattern of Health

When someone is really low and unwell they quickly forget how it feels to be healthy and full of energy, because it's easy to give in to weak energy, which has a low frequency. When someone has been unwell for months or years they have usually become so used to feeling and believing a certain way that it takes consistent work to show them that their situation and body have changed. They will often turn to 'quick fixes' like taking tablets, and it's harder, but much more successful, to get them to work on themselves and their energy. If you wanted to run for a long time, for example, you could take lots of strength-enhancing or energy-boosting drugs and you would keep going, but then you would undoubtedly crash. The better – but more challenging – option would be to become a master of your own body and mind, to listen to your instincts and recognize your needs.

If you have been unwell for a long time, when you get better, you have to change your pattern of thinking. The key thing is to reprogram your mind to match your new healthy body, both now and in the future. You can do this by getting clear about what you want out of life – your ambitions, goals and dreams. You need to see yourself in the future doing what you want and having what you want and build your beliefs so that you can accept the progress you're making.

Imagine Yourself in Good Health

As with many other things in life, you get what you focus on. So you have to be aware of your focus and what you are attracting.

The hardest and the most important thing to change is the pressure that you put yourself under or may RECEIVE from other people. Even if you have a serious condition, you have to focus on positive images so that you don't SEND negative energy that can affect your immune and nervous systems. You need to respect your body when it's not well and care for it and love it even more:

- See light going through your body, making everything shine brightly.

- Imagine water flowing through you, cleansing all your cells and washing out any negative energy.

These powerful thoughts will shift your frequency to the frequency of your condition. But if you see yourself in the future losing your hair, wasting away, not being able to walk, lying in a hospital bed and being too weak to recover, you are actually programming yourself *not* to recover. You cannot do this. You have to see what you *want* to see in the future – yourself doing well, being healthy and being successful. You need to have nourishing thoughts and treat your body in the best way you can. You have to detach yourself from the illness. Then every day you will start to move closer to what you want because you'll be SENDING messages to yourself about how to behave.

Whatever your condition, you need to *always* see yourself better – and really believe it. I've heard many people say 'I'm really positive' as they have a look of total fear on their face and their voice is quaking. If what you say and what you feel don't match, the negative energy will CANCEL the positive energy, so you have to see and feel yourself being healthy.

Some people say that they find it hard to visualize, but it's just like daydreaming and everybody knows how to do that. Here are some points on how to see yourself better:

- Find a quiet place where you won't be disturbed.

- Breathe deeply and try to empty your mind.

- Think about how you want to see yourself in the future – first of all in one month's time ... then in two months' time ... then in six months' time. See yourself walking, having lots of energy, sleeping well and having fun.

- Then imagine how you want to be in a year's time: working, being successful, enjoying life with your family and friends, and feeling even better than before.

- Then think about how you want to be in two years'... and even five years' time. Do you have a new job? A new home? Maybe you've started a family. All the time think about the positive things you want and how you are well enough to do them.

- Then come back from the future to the present.

When you do this you SEND a message to the universe about what you want to have and how you want to feel. You program yourself to be able to go for all of these things in the present and bring the energy of good health to the present too.

You can also change your energy by remembering how your body used to be. Just as you can feel fantastic by remembering times from your past when you were happy and free, so you can return to the memories of good health. This helps to reset the mind to a healthy frequency by re-energizing the frequency of the healthy memory so that you can bring this into the present. Regardless of how long you've been ill, your memories of health are stronger and have lasted longer than your memory of bad health. You need to CANCEL the memory of that illness and engage with the memories of being well. (You cannot CANCEL the memories of being healthy.) You can recover simply by thinking of the times when you were healthy and full of positive energy.

One of my patients was suffering with MS and had reached a point where he was finding it hard to walk. He was very upset and depressed and his family was also suffering watching his decline. He told me that he used to be an athlete, so he found it particularly hard to cope with his body not being able to do what it used to.

I said to him, 'You are still an athlete. You've been an athlete for many more years than you've had this condition.' I got him to start reliving his memories of being fit and strong and being able to walk easily. He brought the powerful positive memories from his past to the present and then he started being himself again. This made it much easier for me to treat him.

If you don't shift your mindset, you can drag yourself back into the frequency of your illness. But you have been fully well before and so you already know how to be well – you just need to practise again.

It's Just a Word...

I've noticed that as soon as we 'label' something as being a particular condition, it makes it much easier for our body to give in to it. So, unless I absolutely have to, I avoid telling my patients about their problems. I just talk about 'blockages' and focus my attention on clearing their energy. You wouldn't believe how many people are disappointed by this! Many people want to be given a long list of ailments and to be able to 'label' every single symptom. They want to justify what they're feeling. A few people even enjoy being victims of their condition, but by attaching themselves to it, they only make it worse.

Also, because of the prevalence of technology, many people rush to look up their symptoms or condition on the internet rather than take the time to listen to their own body and what it is telling them. But because some symptoms can apply to many conditions, it can be easy to be influenced by the information and the suggestions and convince yourself that you're ill – sometimes even when you're not.

There was a highly publicized story recently about a Spanish woman who was diagnosed with ovarian cancer. She was told by her doctors that she had two months to live – and two months later she died. When the post-mortem was done, there was no sign of cancer.

This tragic story proves how powerful labels and suggestion can be: even though this woman was in good health, she weakened her body because she believed she was ill.

Rather than talk about their condition, I always tell people just to relax and go to a peaceful space, because it's much better if I don't communicate anything to them that could create blockages to the energy. You can travel to any frequency you want by thinking about it, and by doing this, your mind SENDS the energetic messages to every cell in your body.

As well as illnesses themselves having a particular energy, labels also carry with them a very powerful energy, so you need to stop finding comfort in being diagnosed and the labels that go with that: you need to CANCEL the frequency of those conditions to protect yourself from the negative energy. You can't allow yourself to tune into the frequency of illness: you have to start observing and emotionally detaching yourself from it to allow your mind to make the right decisions and the healing to take place more quickly.

A Practical Guide to Having a Neutral Attitude to Good Health

When you think or talk about the negative aspects of an illness, or if you think about it all the time, you stop yourself from being in a NEUTRAL state. Instead you build up the frequency of your condition and don't let your body and mind see the way out of it.

You need to control your thoughts and deal with your condition, not give in to it. The things you have to do are:

- If you are unwell or have some symptoms, stop looking up information on the internet. By connecting to this information – some of which won't be true and some of which may not apply to you – you are connecting to the frequency of the illness.

- The same applies to books and articles: if you can't distance yourself from the information, stop reading about the illness.

- Become an outside observer. Step outside your body. Try to imagine you are looking at a friend's body. What can you see? What would you tell them to do to get better? Do they need to eat more healthily? Rest? Relax? When you have the answers, you need to apply them to yourself. As a detached observer, you will make the best decisions for yourself.

- Find a new focus like playing the guitar, cooking, watching comedies, reading love stories or going to the gym, or even book a holiday. Basically, stop looking for illness and no longer agree to be a part of it.

- Try not to talk about your condition. You don't want people to feel sorry for you. Find new topics of conversation that shift you to a positive healthy energy.

- Treat your body with respect. Listen to everything that is best for you. This may include recommendations from your doctors, taking medication and/or making lifestyle changes. For example, although some people who are suffering from cancer choose not to have chemotherapy, many do. But they can also combine this with other changes such as having a healthier diet, relaxing, going out in the sunshine and doing the things they enjoy. These are things you should do because you know they'll help you get better.

When you are in the right state of mind from the start, you will attract the right people, doctors and treatments to help you get better – and you will make the right decisions. Good health always starts in your head.

CHAPTER 11

You Can Transform Your Future

We have now worked our way through the whole energy pyramid and you should be able to see how powerful your mind is. You will also be able to see that you can totally transform your life by paying attention to your energy frequency and the energy around you. So we've covered the theory and also seen lots of examples of how you can SEND and RECEIVE messages to protect yourself and attract what is right for you. Now it's time for you to put this into practice and create the future you want.

Although you will probably have already started changing how you think and noticing the energy frequencies around you, this chapter draws together a series of exercises so you can create a personal action plan to put into practice what you already know. Having these exercises in one place means you can refer back to them whenever you need to.

We'll begin with some general exercises that help you to focus your mind and put into practice the concepts in this book. These are followed by summaries of what we've covered, with an emphasis on what *you* need to do to transform your future.

We're going to start with Energy Breathing because this helps you to move energy in your body and so provides a good foundation for all of this work.

Energy Breathing

Breathing has been recognized as an important element in self-care for a long time and in many cultures. The fact that so many people across the world have practised breathing exercises for many years proves how vital your breath is to achieving a healthy balanced mind and body. It also helps you to achieve a NEUTRAL state.

You have energy in every part of your body and from feeling energy move inside people I have learned that there are certain set energy paths through the body. Energy breathing helps you to move your energy along those paths so that you can keep your frequency strong and in balance.

If you spend a lot of time thinking or concentrating, this breathing will help to ground you and connect you to your body. And if you're always on the run, the stillness of the exercise will help you to relax. Remember your body and mind are connected, and energy breathing is the perfect exercise to bring the two elements closer together to help you find NEUTRAL MIND.

How to Focus Your Mind

It's simple to describe how to energy breathe, but harder to achieve a state of relaxation deep enough to do it well. So you have to start by training your mind to focus. Once you can focus well, your body and mind will automatically relax and help your breathing. These next two exercises are ones I always give people to start them off.

THE MUSIC EXERCISE

Find a piece of music that is played by two instruments, for example a violin and a piano. Listen to it for a while and just appreciate it.

Second time around, pick out one instrument that you want to follow, for example the violin. The aim is for you to block out the other instrument so you can only hear the violin.

I find that the easiest way to do this is to imagine that the violin is someone you really care about – a child, relative, partner or a close friend. By connecting that instrument with your emotions and your thoughts, you will find it easier to focus on it and hold on to it. If you do this well enough, the sound of the other instrument will start to disappear.

Then play the piece through again and listen to the other instrument – in this example, the piano. Again, think of the sound of this instrument as a person you care about and follow its sound. You will start to notice that your mind separates the two sounds and it seems as if you are listening to them using different sides of your head.

The point of this exercise is to relax your mind and put your focus on one area. It can be exhausting to have a busy mind, so it's important to rest it in simple ways. There is so much going on in your body and mind at any one time that you need to be able to achieve a Zen-like state where your mind is clear. With practice, this exercise can help you recognize and switch off from the constant 'background music' that you often absorb and process without even being aware of it.

THE CIRCLES EXERCISE

For the second exercise you need to use the pictures below. You will see that both are of two concentric circles, but that Figure A has a black inner circle and a white outer one and Figure B has a black outer circle and a white inner one.

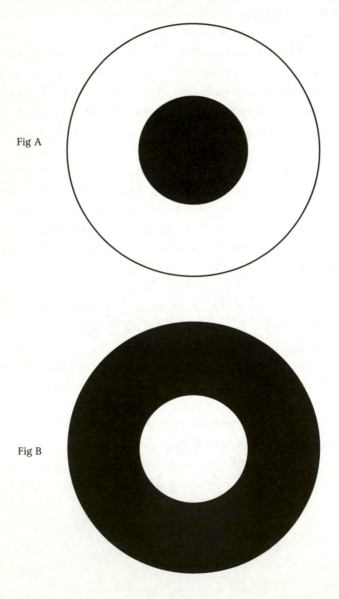

Fig A

Fig B

The first thing to do is to cover Figure B with a piece of paper, or anything that takes it out of your sight line. Make sure you are relaxed and sitting comfortably in a quiet space.

- Look at Figure A. Do not stare too hard, just gently allow your eyes to relax and see the image.

- After a minute or so, close your eyes. You should still be able to see the image vividly in your mind's eye, but it will appear in the opposite shades: the outer white circle will appear black and the inner black circle will appear white. It is like looking at a photograph and then looking at its negative.

- Once you have managed to hold this image in your mind's eye for a while, open your eyes and look back at Figure A.

- Again look gently at the image for a short time and then close your eyes.

- This time, although your mind's eye will show you an image that looks like Figure B, try to reverse the image so that you see the original image in Figure A – the white outer circle and the black inner circle.

- Once you can recall the actual image of Figure A from memory, hold it in your mind's eye for as long as you can.

Although this sounds simple, for many people it can take a lot of practice to perfect this reversal technique. You need to train your mind to memorize the image as you actually saw it, rather than the reversed image that your mind wants to see.

This exercise helps you to reverse the way you see things, so that you can look beyond what might seem like a negative situation and see the positive things around you instead. It helps you to stand back and observe what is going on, rather than reacting to it – so that you can stay NEUTRAL regardless of what is happening.

If you have the ability to turn around your feelings, you can protect yourself from negative frequencies. This isn't always easy to do, but even though it takes a lot of attention, it can be very relaxing.

General Guidelines for Energy Breathing

For these exercises you need to sit somewhere quiet and comfortable where you can be at peace for a few minutes. The beauty of these exercises is their simplicity and although you need to focus, you'll find them easier with practice.

Before you start, here are a few guidelines:

- Sit or lie down in a quiet and comfortable place where you can be at peace for a few minutes. Make sure that you won't be disturbed. I find that a sitting position is best, because you're more likely to stay awake.

- When you breathe in, draw the breath down into your diaphragm (just below your rib cage). This helps you to breathe as deeply as possible and to avoid shallow breaths.

- You may choose to listen to music – it's your choice. If you do, make sure it has a gentle rhythm that matches the pace of slow breathing.

- You will probably find it easiest to do these exercises with your eyes shut. This will help you shut out any distractions and you can focus on what's happening inside your body.

- Adopt an open position with your arms and legs uncrossed. This keeps your energy channels open.

- When you have been breathing and visualizing energy for a few minutes, you may start to feel energized and even perhaps a little buzzy. This is due in part to the increase in oxygen in the brain but is also due to the movement of your energy. So, after you have finished, spend a few moments relaxing and bring your attention to your surroundings. Energy breathing can be very powerful and a few minutes of it can cause you to feel light-headed if you're not used to it. When you're ready, get up slowly and steadily.

Preparation for Energy Breathing

The usual path of your breath is through your nose or mouth and down into your lungs, where the oxygen is passed into the bloodstream to be transported around the body. Energy breathing is different. Whilst you're doing these exercises, I want you to forget where oxygen goes and just think of where your *energy* is moving. To help you with this, there is a visual element to the exercises.

A PREPARATORY EXERCISE

This first exercise takes a few moments. It helps you to connect with all the parts of your body and is simply a precursor to full-body breathing.

- Start by breathing deeply through your nose for a few moments.

- Turn your full attention to your body by focusing on each part in turn. Start with your toes. Put your attention into them and notice how they feel. They may start to tingle with energy or they may feel heavy with relaxation.

- Once you have felt your awareness fully in your toes, turn your attention in the same way to your ankles.

- Once you feel your awareness there, move on to your calves and knees and so on, working your way upwards through each part of the body.

Once you've done this and your breathing is deep and steady, you can do a specific exercise.

BASIC ENERGY BREATHING

This form of breathing is the best to help you get into a meditative state and is also good at energizing you.

- As you inhale, imagine energy entering your body through the base of your spine, which some people call the root chakra.

- As you breathe in, let this energy travel up your body as far as your solar plexus. It may help to imagine the energy as a colour or light travelling through you.

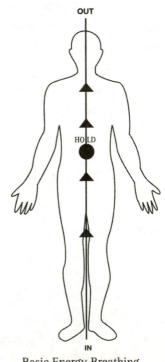

Basic Energy Breathing

- Hold your breath at your solar plexus for three seconds.

- Now as you exhale, gently push the energy up through your body and out of the crown of your head.

Repeat this pattern of breathing for as long as you feel comfortable, up to 30 minutes.

DOUBLE T FULL-BODY BREATHING

This exercise is very good for cleansing and energizing your kidneys, liver and heart.

- As you inhale, imagine energy entering your body through the base of your spine, which some people call the root chakra.

- As you breathe in, let this energy travel up your body as far as your solar plexus. It may help to imagine the energy as a colour or light travelling through you.

- As you exhale, gently push the energy out of the sides of your body, as if it is going through your liver, stomach and kidneys.

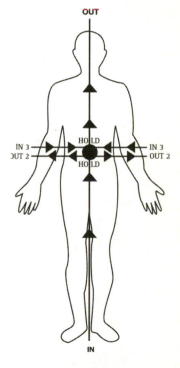

Double T Breathing

- On the next breath in, bring the energy back to your solar plexus and hold it there for three seconds.

- Now as you exhale, gently push the energy up through your body and out of the crown of your head.

Repeat this pattern of breathing for as long as you feel comfortable, up to 30 minutes.

FULL-BODY BREATHING

This is the main energy breathing exercise that I teach people. It's fantastic for general self-healing – mental and physical – and it's something I always do in my seminars because the perfect time to teach people is when I have them in front of me. I always enjoy doing this myself because it feels so good, and you'll see how powerful it is. As with all energy breathing exercises, this exercise is a form of meditation as, in my opinion, meditation is about being in control of your mind, your energy and your soul.

- Start to breathe through your nose as deeply and smoothly as you can.

- Once you feel relaxed, as you breathe in, imagine energy entering the base of your spine, also known as the root chakra.

- With your intention, send the energy up the spine.

- As you breathe out, let the energy leave your body through the crown of the head. Repeat this cycle a few times. This is the main path of energy through the body and it brings the universal energy into your body through the spinal cord.

- On the next cycle of breaths, move the energy up through the root chakra and up the spine as before, but let it leave the body through the centre of your forehead, just above your eyes. This area is known as the third eye.

- On the next cycle, send the energy out through the throat. Repeat this a few times, remembering to breathe deeply throughout.

- Move on to let the energy out through the heart chakra. At each stage, breathe deeply through any discomfort or resistance you might feel.

- Start the next cycle as the others, but this time let the energy exit the body through the solar plexus.

- The last cycle of breaths sends the energy out through the sacral chakra, which is just below your navel.

- Once you have completed all six cycles, spend a few moments centring yourself before you move.

This exercise moves energy all around the main energy channels and helps to clear out the body whilst giving the mind a break too. It's safe for everyone to do and you can focus on areas in the body that you know need the most attention.

The Practical Side of Neutrality

When you put yourself in an energetic state that is balanced, NEUTRAL and strong, you are a huge step closer to having the life you want. When you vibrate at this frequency, not only can you think, see and feel clearly, but you can also attract what is right for you and take action to create it.

We all have an intuitive sense of what we should be doing with our lives and what's best for us, but we don't always pay attention to it. Your energy is like your navigation system: when you're on the right track, it vibrates strongly, and when you veer off, it shifts. That's the time to do something about it, but to recognize when this is happening, you need to be in NEUTRALITY.

It is much easier to be in NEUTRALITY if you are in a good physical state. Many of these tips are things that you will probably be familiar with as general health suggestions, but you may not realize that they affect your frequency too:

- Take regular exercise.

- Spend time outdoors and get fresh air as often as you can.

- Drink lots of water and herbal teas.

- Limit your caffeine and alcohol intake.

- Avoid nicotine and any other drugs.

- Get a good night's sleep so you feel refreshed.

- Eat a diet that is rich in fruit, vegetables and good-quality protein.

- Limit your intake of carbohydrates that release energy quickly into your body, for example white bread and white rice.

- Limit sugary and junk foods.

- Do regular relaxation or meditation exercises.

By taking care of yourself you show that you respect yourself and your energy will be stronger and more balanced, making it easier for you to attract what you want. For your life to be transformed, you have to be ready both physically and mentally.

Know What You Need

When you can listen to your feelings and control your own mind, you will be able to recognize what you need in your future. Be excited about your ambitions and your dreams, and don't just think about them, but notice how you feel when you imagine them really happening.

Let's take some simple examples:

- If you really want to go skiing, you need to see yourself doing it. And when your mind can see that happening, it becomes programmed to get you there and so you attract the right energy to get what you need. You will then attract enough money, the right level of fitness and the right resort for you.

- If you want to start a new business, you should see it being successful and plan how to get there: imagine finding the right method of finance, visualize the people to help you set it up and the best premises, and then imagine lots of customers being attracted to it.

- If you want a new house, you need to see yourself moving into the house of your dreams. Be excited about saving money, see yourself getting a promotion or pay rise to help pay for it and see yourself finding the right home quickly and without any hiccups.

- If you want a new job, you have to see yourself already in it. Then you will start to look for new opportunities, think about training yourself for any new skills you might need and imagine going through the interview process confidently and competently.

You need to see *and* feel your goals. You also need to believe they will come to you and really try to feel them happening so you can see how they will feel when they do.

See the Life You Want

Once you've started to get in touch with what you want by being in NEUTRALITY, you can do this very powerful exercise to help you focus on the future. By doing this you train your mind to be there as if what you want *has already happened*:

FOCUSING ON THE FUTURE

- Find a quiet place to sit where you won't be disturbed for at least five minutes.

- Think of something that you want to happen in the future. Make sure it's a positive image and something that you really want. Check that your energy and instinct feel right when you think about it. If you are in any doubt at all or you get a hunch that it isn't right for you, pay attention to what your intuition is telling you and change whatever you need to change to make it feel correct.

- When this feels clear and motivating, imagine you're in that situation now. Use all of your senses to experience what you'll see and hear and how you'll feel once you've reached your goal.

- Stay in the future experience for a few minutes or until you start to feel your energy change. You may feel strong or excited, as if you know this will really happen.

- When you feel ready, bring your attention back to the present and take a few moments to orient yourself.

When you do this exercise, you are preparing yourself for what you want. You can do it for things at any time in the future – weeks, months or years ahead. And when what you want does actually happen, you'll be ready to deal with it and accept it.

Write Down Your Goals

When you really want something and you find NEUTRALITY, you SEND your wish to the universe. It can make a huge difference when you write down what you want, as it helps you to gain clarity and also to focus your mind. Like the woman on page 115 who wrote down the kind of man she wanted to meet *and the date* by which she wanted to meet him, you should be precise with the time you want to achieve your goals.

One of my friends decided that he wanted to move to a mansion. It was a dream he had always had. He could imagine what the mansion would look like and he wrote down what he wanted – how many rooms, what it looked like outside and in, what the garden was like and where it was. He wrote down that he wanted to be living in that house in five years' time. He then put this piece of paper into an envelope, wrote the date of five years in the future on the outside, put it in a drawer and forgot about it.

Over the next few years he attracted the right job, made money and saved up. He moved house with his family, and as they were unpacking boxes in his new home, he came across the sealed envelope. It was the date that he had written on the outside. He then remembered that he'd written down his dream and when he opened up and read what he'd put down all those years ago, he found that, down to the last detail, he was now in his dream mansion. What he had wished for five years before had come true.

This is a very simple yet powerful exercise and can be really enjoyable to do. And *as well as* or *instead of* writing down what you want, you can also do it in a visual way by collecting pictures of your goals and making a collage of your future. Some people call this a Treasure Map.

One New Year, I decided that I would focus my attention that year on really getting what I wanted out of my life. I found a big piece of cardboard and started looking through some old magazines to find inspiring pictures.

One of the things I knew I really wanted was a luxurious holiday and I found a picture in a travel magazine of a beautiful stretch of beach with a lovely hotel in the background. I didn't know where it was, but it looked perfect. I hung it up on my bedroom wall and after a while I forgot it was there.

A couple of months later, my husband and I started looking into holidays and I left it up to him to organize. He came back from work one day all excited. He told me he'd booked the holiday and showed me the resort in a brochure. It was in Mauritius and looked amazing – and familiar. I ran upstairs to look at the picture on my wall: without even knowing, my husband had booked the dream resort that I had 'chosen'!

You can have fun with this exercise and get creative about how you do it. And, as these stories show, you need to make sure you *really* want what you choose – as you'll be very likely to get it.

Attract What Is Best for You

This next exercise helps you to see the value of being clear about what you want and how that clarity can bring you what you need.

SEEING WHAT YOU WANT TO SEE

- Look at the shapes below.

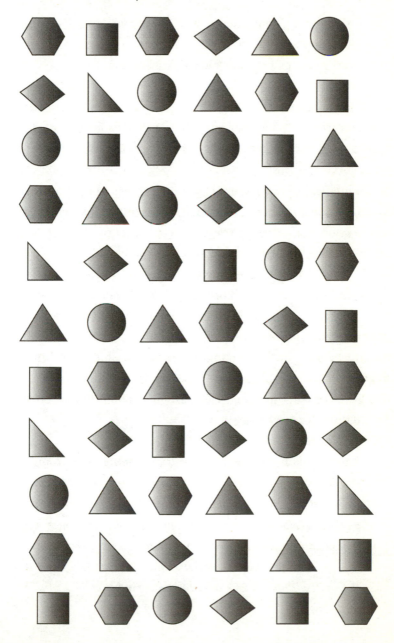

- Now focus on finding all the triangles.

- Then focus on finding all the circles.

- Keep changing the shape that you're trying to find until you've gone through all the shapes: triangle, circle, hexagon, right-angled triangle, square and diamond.

Do you notice how your mind very quickly picks out the shape that you want to see? After a while of looking for one shape only, you will find these start to stand out on the page.

In a similar way, your mind picks out the things in life you decide to look for, and when you open your channels of awareness, you will really start to recognize how your energy changes when you're focused and clear about what you want.

I wonder if you've ever wanted a new car and as soon as you've decided that you want that particular model, you've seen it everywhere. Any woman who's pregnant will start to see pregnant women wherever she looks. Naturally, you start to tune into the things that you're thinking about and so shift to a different frequency and start attracting those things, whether they are job opportunities, the right house, a particular quality in a person – or coins, as this next story shows:

One day my partner and I were at a supermarket and had just finished shopping. Out of the blue, she said to me, 'I'm going to find a pound coin.' She was so sure it was going to happen. She walked over to the trolleys and, sure enough, came back with a pound coin. You may be thinking that this happens quite a lot in supermarkets because you use pound coins as a deposit on the trolley. But this was only the beginning...

A few months later, more money started appearing. In fact it seemed that wherever we went, money appeared. It was weird – and not at all normal for us. On one occasion my parents-in-law were staying with us and we took them to our local garden centre. We told them about all the coins we'd been finding since we'd started seeing Seka for treatment and my partner's mum found this very amusing. I'm not sure she believed us. We got out of the car and within ten steps my partner found a 20p coin lying on the floor. We all burst out laughing!

A few weeks later, my partner joked that we only ever found coins and that it was about time we started finding notes. We thought nothing more of it because she was only joking. Later that day, she went to the supermarket and came home with a big smile on her face. She'd found a £5 note!

Coins were appearing so frequently by that time that we started to write down whenever we found them. So I can safely report that in the past 12 months we have found a total of 44 coins and one banknote. What's interesting, though, is that if we consciously look, we find nothing. Our discoveries nearly always happen unexpectedly. Also, we always thank the universe and give double the amount of our findings to charity. Maybe this is why we keep on attracting money!

This story shows that it's amazing what you can find when you put your attention on it. By setting your frequency to a particular thing, you are more likely to attract it.

Match Your Intention with Action

You can't just dream, though, and wait for everything to land in your lap! Once you have sent a message to the universe about what you want, you need to stop thinking about it and start opening yourself up to using your abilities and creativity in the right way. In the earlier example, the man who dreamed of living in a mansion made sure he worked hard to build up his business and do well for himself in order to afford his dream: he didn't do this consciously, but his subconscious knew what he really wanted to achieve.

Often you have to stretch yourself to aim for goals that seem slightly out of your reach. As the next story shows, when you do this with a positive intention, the universe will provide for you:

I used to live next door to an actress. Although she had been working for many years, she had only ever landed small parts. When we were chatting one day she told me that she had seen a house she really loved but she couldn't afford it because she didn't have enough work. I told her to stretch herself and imagine that she would get enough work and money to pay for that lovely home. She said she'd never thought that way before and something in her shifted.

She set her heart and intention on that house and within a few months she got several job offers, one of which was a key role in a major television series. She managed to buy her dream house.

When you extend your energy, everything will follow and opportunities will come to you.

The world does not automatically put you on the right path, of course; you have to find it, and the way to do this is to pay attention to all the signs you RECEIVE from the Super-Subconscious. Remember that coincidences are more than chance happenings – they are signs that you're being SENT a message and you need to listen to it.

Finding the Right Relationships

As I said in Chapter 9, you need to be aware of the energy you SEND to other people and RECEIVE from them. By doing this you can recognize whether the people in your life are right for you.

If you have come out of a relationship, whether or not it was what you wanted at the time, you have to see it as being a positive thing for you now. Think about the things that person didn't have or do. Maybe they didn't make you laugh. Maybe they stopped being intimate with you. Perhaps they didn't support you or they made you feel inferior. There will always be a reason why you *could* and *should* have someone better. The kinds of things that may be helpful for you to think in this situation are:

- 'It's better this happened now before we got married/had children/bought a house.'

- 'It's better I found this out before I spent the rest of my life with them.'

- 'It's better for both of us because now we will attract the people that we need and deserve, the people that are right for us.'

When you see all the reasons why splitting up was the right thing for both of you, you will find it easier to let go and move on – and this will give you the space to attract someone else.

Finally, if you are particularly looking for a partner, remember to write down all of the things you want in someone – the things that are most important to *you* and that will make you happy. You need to think about how you want the person to act, what you want them to look like and all the other qualities you find attractive. You should also write down where you want to be with that person and imagine yourself in all those places with them. You need to see the life you want to have and who you want to have it with in as much detail as you can.

You can also visualize this, which can help you get used to the feeling of being with the right person and knowing deep down that it will happen:

BEING WITH THE RIGHT PERSON

- Find a quiet place to sit where you won't be disturbed for at least five minutes.

- Think of the person you want to be with in the future. Make sure it's a positive image and somebody who you really want. You can check that your energy and instinct feel right when you think about it. If you are in any doubt or you get a hunch that that person isn't right for you, pay attention to what your intuition is telling you and change whatever you need to change about them to feel good.

- When this feels clear and motivating, imagine you're with that person now. Use all of your senses to experience what you'll see and hear and how you'll feel.

- Stay in the future experience of being in that relationship for a few minutes or until you start to feel your energy change. You may feel strong or excited, as if you know this will really happen.

- When you feel ready, bring your attention back to the present and take a few moments to orient yourself.

How to Protect Yourself

When you are around people who carry a draining energy, like those who are *always* depressed, have a negative attitude to life or thrive on things going wrong, you need to be careful. When groups of people get together to share a negative energy, the 'pull' can be particularly strong, but, as with any situation you find yourself in, you are always in control of your own reactions. You don't have to join in. Sometimes people say that they are particularly 'sensitive' to certain energies, but you have to step back from this sensitivity and be an observer of it rather than getting sucked into it. You always have a choice. Being sensitive is actually a gift because you can sense when something is wrong and so decide to step out of it.

It's quite common to find this kind of negative 'pull' in work environments, where people often like to huddle together to complain. They might moan about their boss, the demands of their job or other people in the office, but rarely does any good come from this kind of 'group negativity'.

If you are in this kind of situation, the best thing you can do for yourself is step back, be NEUTRAL and observe what is going on. By detaching yourself, you will be protected from the draining energy. You don't have to be like everyone else. You can always be your own person.

When you are aware of the frequencies around you and what your gut is telling you, you are already starting to protect yourself. Once you are aware of the signs you are getting, you can make a choice about what to do, whom to spend time with and how to react to what's going on around you.

How to Be in the Best of Health

Just as each of us has a different level of ability in things like sport and music, so each of us has our own level of healing ability. Whilst very few people can heal others with a lot of success, what we can all do is pay attention to our own energy to take care of our health and self-healing.

You need to notice how your energy gets affected by things around you – people, places etc. When you do get drained? When do you feel most alive? What are the signs that you need to take a rest? What are your weak points – the first things to show that you're run down? Maybe you get a sore throat, or your skin flares up, or you can't digest food properly, or you can't sleep at night. We are all different, and so are our limitations, so you need to tune into your own energy and get to know what happens for you when life gets tough.

Once you become aware of your boundaries, you can learn to say 'no' to things that take you away from your healthy frequency. Your health comes first, even if part of your life involves caring for others. You cannot look after other people unless you are strong and healthy, so accept that when you say 'no' to someone else, you're actually saying 'yes' to yourself. Be clear on who you are and what you can do.

On the flip side, you also need to notice what things make you feel most alive. This might include playing a musical instrument or singing, walking up a mountain, being by the sea, spending time with your children, partner, friends or family, or doing something artistic like sculpting, drawing, painting or gardening. By recognizing and then doing these things, you help to keep your frequency strong and in tune and this is how you can stay healthy in the long term.

Love and Respect Your Body

If you are unwell or in pain you need to love and respect your body even more than when you are well. Also, if there is a part of your body that is not working well or that you really don't like, you need to give attention to this part more than all the others:

- Tell each part of yourself that you love and appreciate it

- If you're not unwell but you just don't like your body (maybe because you think you're too fat or too thin), make sure to say lovely things to it.

- Give positive attention to all of yourself as often as you can.

When you look after a garden, you tend to the plants that are dying or wilting and that need most care. If you are caring for or teaching children, you give more attention to the ones who are struggling or are left out. You need to do this for your body too; don't ignore the parts of yourself that need your love and attention the most.

The Frequency of Words

Because language, both written and spoken, is so important in our world, it helps to use the right words to attract what you want. Just as objects, people, places, thoughts and feelings have their own frequencies, so do words.

You can see how powerful a word can be when you look at how people respond to an illness. For example, if someone finds out they've got cancer, that one word can instil so much fear and negative emotion that it can make them attract that negative frequency when what they really want is to get rid of it.

WORDS AND ENERGY

Choose words that make you feel good and that make your energy feel strong. Try saying the words on the list below and notice how you feel inside.

LOVE   PEACE   FUN
FLOW
ENERGY   STRENGTH
OCEAN
CALM   LAUGHTER
CREATIVITY   CUDDLES   FLOWERS
SUNSHINE   WARMTH   SMILE
NATURE   PASSION   ENERGY
SKY   JOY   COMPASSION
MELODY   PLEASURE   FRAGRANCE
GRASS
NATURE   COMFORT   BABY
GOODNESS   HAPPINESS
BEAUTY   KISS   MELODY
KINDNESS
GIGGLE   LOVER   WARMTH
HEALTH

I'm not even going to write down any negative words, but I'm sure you already know how these make you feel. When you are doing this exercise, think about the words that make you feel the best.

Even though words are important, just saying them won't get you the full positive benefit. Whilst words do carry an energy, when you also have the belief and intention of whatever the word is, you'll make that energy so much more powerful and compelling.

You can have a play with this idea by saying 'I love you', but saying it when you feel really angry inside. Then imagine the face of someone you love deeply and again say 'I love you.' Notice how the quality of the energy – both of the words and inside you – changes with your intention.

Some scientists have even researched the effect of words on our health. One of the best-known researchers in this area is a Japanese man called Masaru Emoto. He and his team wrote words on pieces of paper, taped these to glasses of water and left them overnight. The structure of the water molecules was compared before and after, and the researchers found that negative phrases and words caused the molecules to disintegrate and become unstable, whereas positive phrases, such as 'Love and appreciation' and 'Thank you' made them hold healthy patterns. Our bodies are made up of between 55 and 75 per cent water and so our cells are affected by the frequency of words in a similar way to the water molecules.

The Frequency of Colour

Descriptive words have energy too, and colour words are something that you can play around with. If you decide to focus on the word 'red' and look around you, for example, you will start to notice everything that is red. Then you can choose a different colour and see how many things around you are of that colour.

This shows you how your mind quickly is programmed to recognize something you are focused on. Also, you will notice how you can spot the tiniest bits of the colour you are focusing on – you will see it everywhere.

You can use this exercise to connect with a colour that has a positive association for you. So if, for example, green makes you feel strong, you can look for this everywhere and it will make you feel stronger. If red makes you think of love, or you associate blue with calm and peace, you can choose to find this all around you. You can also program your mind to look for a colour word and then to associate that with something positive.

How to Find Your Perfect Career

How many people do you know who genuinely love what they do? How many people look forward to going to work because they're proud of what they achieve? I know lots of people who dislike their work, and a dreary job can be a major cause of stress. I've found that many people aren't in the most suitable jobs for them and a lot of the time their body is telling them it's not right, but they just don't read the signs.

When you do a job that doesn't use your natural strengths or you work for a person or organization whose ethics are very different from yours, your energy will be telling you that it's not right: you will get a sense of dis-ease, like a churning stomach, a knot in your heart, an energy crash, headaches or a stiff back. These signs are telling you that your frequency is off-track and that you need to pay attention to it. You have to find the job that matches your energy. If you don't match your energy to the right profession, even if you are making enough money to live on, you will become unwell because you're not using your energy as you should.

When you are looking for a career or to change job, you need to be sure that you are following a path for the right reasons and find your own gift, regardless of what anyone else says or does. When you recognize your ability and creativity – and use them – you are being true to yourself. You feed yourself with your own energy because you are doing what you love and what you were born to do. You also feel healthier and happier and attract positive things into your life because your frequency is where it should be.

Many years ago, I treated a very successful lawyer. Even though he was very good at what he did, he was tired, unhappy and couldn't see his future. He was depressed without knowing why. He stayed in this negative state until he realized that he was not following his dream: what he had always wanted to do was paint. We discussed this and he realized that he had nothing to lose by giving it a go. He was wealthy and so could afford to paint for a year – and then if it didn't work out, he could always go back to the law.

As it turned out, he made a success of his new career and is now a recognized painter. He is healthy, happy and has now also started a family. When he changed his career to suit himself, his whole life changed too.

To transform your own life in a similar way, you have to find the best in yourself and use it to make yourself healthy and happy. How do you do it?

Think Back to Your Childhood

The best way to get in touch with your natural talents is to think back to what you used to love doing when you were a child, because we don't change that much when we grow up. Whether you loved playing with cars, being a nurse, teaching your teddy bears or cooking things with your mum, there will have been something that made you feel good.

We all have things that we naturally do well and when each of us works with these talents we find that we fit together like a jigsaw. No particular talent stands out as more important than another – they're just different. Anyone who has ever had a job that didn't suit them will be able to relate to this. Whether you took that job because you needed the money or you made a mistake and thought you were doing the right thing, you'll remember what it felt like to try and fit into a role that simply wasn't suited to you. I'd guess that you weren't happy when you were doing this. But the dangerous thing is believing that this is normal: this is *not* normal, nor is it natural. It's natural to discover what you really, really want to do and what you are best suited to do rather than following someone else's path.

Retirement

A happy work life is not just about finding the right career but also about ending your career in the healthiest way. When people retire, it's not just their working life that is affected – everything from their body to their mind is impacted. Some people even find it hard to say 'I'm going to retire' because they see it as an ending, or a full stop.

Rather than seeing retirement as an ending, you have to see it as a new beginning. It is a time of freedom. After working hard for many years, you now have time to travel, see friends and family, work on your hobbies or maybe start a new career. Whatever you do, don't sit still and put yourself in a box. Your age is irrelevant and you need to keep your mind active and focused on the positive, whatever stage of life you're at. You can use all the experiences you've had to date to start again – and the opportunities can be endless. Even some people in their seventies and eighties keep their mind and body active. They feel good still being energized and busy, and often turn their energies to help others.

Think Yourself Young

We're all told that as we get older, we also get weaker and that our cells die, but we can change this. After a certain age, everybody wants to be younger and healthier, so why don't we think ourselves younger? If we can change this programming, we can slow down the ageing process; by telling ourselves we are getting younger, we can change the frequency in our body:

- With every birthday, tell yourself in your head that you are actually becoming younger by one year. (You don't need to tell people what you are doing, only to think it in your own mind.)

- Be happy with your age, whatever the number, because you're making yourself younger with your thoughts.

By doing this you SEND a message through your NEUTRAL MIND to your body and it will start to behave as you ask it to. And by acting younger, your body will become healthier.

Balance Your Life

So far we have looked at three of the main areas in life – relationships, health and career – but something I often see is people who are *very* successful in one of these areas but pay *no* attention to other areas. For example, they may have reached the pinnacle of their career but aren't very happy in their private life. Or they are secure in their relationship but their health is poor.

Often the people who find it hardest to find balance in their life are those who are very talented at what they do professionally. But your talent is just your talent – it is not you. So, whatever your gift, whether you are an athlete, an actress or a business person, when you stop doing your 'day job' you need to move your focus to the other areas of your life so your energy will be healthier and your life more balanced. What you have to do is take what you do in your professional life and apply it to your personal life to balance out your energy. This exercise will help you to do that:

CREATING BALANCE

- Recognize the imbalance between the different areas in your life.

- Focus on the one area where you are most successful.

- Remember your state of mind when you are in the zone where you perform well and make the best decisions without questioning what you are doing – that state when you know that what you are doing is right.

- Then apply that state of mind and focus to the areas of your life you don't pay enough attention to.

Use Your Past to Move Forward

Your past, good or bad, has made you who you are today. It has also given you the skills and experience that you can draw on to move forward.

Often it is through our problems and difficult times that we learn the most and become stronger, but we can sometimes look back with regret or bitterness. You can't change what happened, but you *can* transform the way you view what happened by only seeing the positive in it, whatever it was. People who have had the hardest lives are often those who go on to have the happiest futures. You can take steps towards a happy future yourself by reversing the negative thoughts in your head. No matter how hard it feels, look for the positive things in a situation. Depending on what that is, you could think:

'Thank goodness I'm not hurt.'

'It's not a big deal. I'll cope with this.'

'At least I'm alive.'

'There is someone better for me.'

'There is a job better suited to me.'

'The right house is out there for me.'

'I caught it just in time.'

'I can learn from this.'

'I can make money again.'

'I may have lost my job, but I still have my family.'

'It wasn't meant to be.'

'I can always have another go.'

You need to recognize the positive in everything and attract that frequency into your life.

Be Grateful

There are many things to be grateful for in our lives and one of the best ways to keep your energy strong is to tap into the frequency of gratitude by regularly giving thanks for what you have. Whether it's your health, family, friends or the food you eat, you can give thanks for it. You can be grateful for life itself, for knowledge and for experience, because these things give you reason to exist. You can also respect the universe for the signs you RECEIVE, because by following these you can make your life better every day.

A Final Word

I don't have the answers to all the world's problems but I do know that the way in which we to choose to live has significant repercussions on how we feel. Every single element of your life affects your energy: the work you do, the people you spend time with, the lifestyle you pursue and the way you think. All of these things are a *choice* and all of these choices have an impact on the vibration of your energy.

To get the most out of life, you need to really know what you want – not what anybody else wants or what you think you want. You are in control of your mind and are the master of your thoughts. You broadcast these thoughts all of the time, so now you can recognize this and make sure that what you broadcast is positive, happy and nourishing.

You can also recognize your own energy shifts and use that knowledge to manage your health and happiness. Remember, you already know how to do this. And when you start to understand and think more widely about these experiences, you can open up to new frequencies. With this knowledge you don't need to rely on computers, phones and other technology to SEND and RECEIVE messages or pictures, as you have these abilities within yourself.

We can all turn negative energy into positive and we can take this gift and use it to change not only ourselves but also the state of our planet. We need to believe that we can make a difference both through what we do on an individual level and by coming together and joining our energies in a powerful way. If we could get everyone in the world to believe that every gesture made a difference, people would be more likely to change their behaviour. We *can* make a huge difference if we create a mass energy of happiness and positivity.

Always remember, *you know more than you think* – and if you haven't recognized this before, hopefully now you do.

So ... now close your eyes and take a deep breath and ...

SEND LOVE

If you are interested in finding out more about Seka's work, or if you would like to book a treatment or attend one of her seminars, please visit:

www.sekanikolic.com

We hope you enjoyed this Hay House book.
If you would like to receive a free catalogue featuring additional
Hay House books and products, or if you would like information
about the Hay Foundation, please contact:

Hay House UK Ltd
292B Kensal Road • London W10 5BE
Tel: (44) 20 8962 1230; Fax: (44) 20 8962 1239
www.hayhouse.co.uk

***

Published and distributed in the United States of America by:
Hay House, Inc. • PO Box 5100 • Carlsbad, CA 92018-5100
Tel: (1) 760 431 7695 or (1) 800 654 5126;
Fax: (1) 760 431 6948 or (1) 800 650 5115
www.hayhouse.com

***

Published and distributed in Australia by:
Hay House Australia Ltd • 18/36 Ralph Street • Alexandria, NSW 2015
Tel: (61) 2 9669 4299, Fax: (61) 2 9669 4144
www.hayhouse.com.au

***

Published and distributed in the Republic of South Africa by:
Hay House SA (Pty) Ltd • PO Box 990 • Witkoppen 2068
Tel/Fax: (27) 11 467 8904
www.hayhouse.co.za

***

Published and distributed in India by:
Hay House Publishers India • Muskaan Complex • Plot No.3
B-2• Vasant Kunj • New Delhi - 110 070
Tel: (91) 11 41761620; Fax: (91) 11 41761630
www.hayhouse.co.in

***

Distributed in Canada by:
Raincoast • 9050 Shaughnessy St • Vancouver, BC V6P 6E5
Tel: (1) 604 323 7100
Fax: (1) 604 323 2600

***

Sign up via the Hay House UK website to receive the Hay House
online newsletter and stay informed about what's going on with your
favourite authors. You'll receive bimonthly announcements
about discounts and offers, special events, product highlights,
free excerpts, giveaways, and more!
www.hayhouse.co.uk

JOIN THE HAY HOUSE FAMILY

As the leading self-help, mind, body and spirit publisher in the UK, we'd like to welcome you to our family so that you can enjoy all the benefits our website has to offer.

 EXTRACTS from a selection of your favourite author titles

 COMPETITIONS, PRIZES & SPECIAL OFFERS Win extracts, money off, downloads and so much more

 LISTEN to a range of radio interviews and our latest audio publications

 CELEBRATE YOUR BIRTHDAY An inspiring gift will be sent your way

 **LATEST NEWS** Keep up with the latest news from and about our authors

 ATTEND OUR AUTHOR EVENTS Be the first to hear about our author events

 iPHONE APPS Download your favourite app for your iPhone

 HAY HOUSE INFORMATION Ask us anything, all enquiries answered

join us online at **www.hayhouse.co.uk**

 292B Kensal Road, London W10 5BE
T: 020 8962 1230 E: info@hayhouse.co.uk

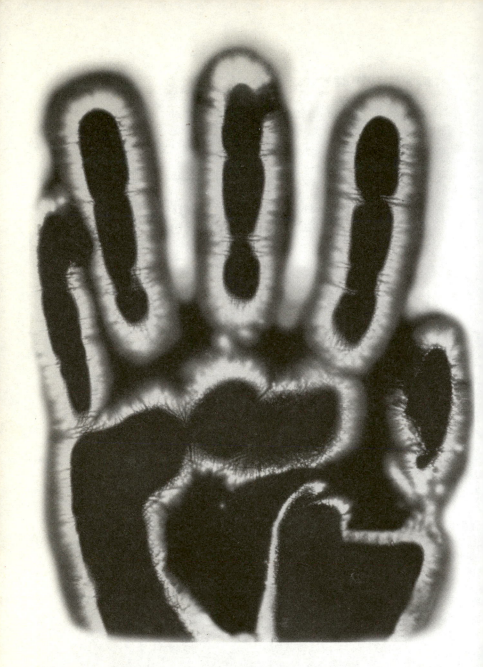

Please feel free to use these electron images of my hands when taking part in my World-wide Distance Healing Events. All dates and details for these events can be found on my website, **www.sekanikolic.com**